The Roadside Scholar

"If your kids or your colleagues roll their eyes when you talk about financial issues, you should keep talking -- but in a different language. That's where *The Roadside Scholar* comes in. Author Brad Stinn tested his teaching methods in front of the toughest audience imaginable: his fellow inmates. Result? New, engaging strategies to keep the attention of surly teenagers -- even as you teach them about money."

– Jonathan Clements, editor of HumbleDollar.com, author of *How to Think About Money* and formerly personal finance columnist for *The Wall Street Journal*

"Brad Stinn's life has taken the most unexpected turns, but he has put his journey to work for the benefit of others -- and produced a book of rare insight and intelligence. There is practical advice here, but also hard-won wisdom."

– Jeffrey Toobin, Chief Legal Analyst CNN, writer New Yorker, author

"I have known Brad since he was a middle schooler. Not only is *The Roadside Scholar* accessible and well-written, it is timely. Students today are starved for real world knowledge and experiences. An understanding of personal finance is no longer a nice extra; it is a fundamental requirement of an educated citizen. I believe we should educate our students holistically; financial health integrates well with physical, emotional and spiritual health in the development of our young men and women into confident and competent adults."

– James Kubacki, President, St. Edward High School

"The Roadside Scholar is a must-read for every high school and college student, parent and grandparent, young and middle-aged worker, entrepreneur and non-profit manager - anyone who would like to have more money in the future than they have now. *The Roadside Scholar* peels back the onion on difficult-to-understand concepts and puts them into easy-to-understand terms. Brad Stinn has given us hands-on, practical advice on what it means to invest and how to do it. I wish I had this book 40 years ago!"

– Jeannee Parker Martin, President & CEO, LeadingAge California

"In 2009, under circumstances that he could not have regretted more, Brad Stinn had time. With that time, he remained a loving husband and father and became an important leader in a worthy cause—helping to cure our citizens, young and old, inmate or non-inmate, of investment illiteracy. In prose that is smart, witty and straightforward, and using real life examples, Brad preaches and teaches the gospel of building wealth. I wish I had read such a book long ago, and will share its wisdom widely with friends and family."

– David C. Scheper, Founder and Chairman, Scheper Kim & Harris LLP, former Criminal Chief of the Los Angeles US Attorney's Office

"Brad Stinn, *The Roadside Scholar*, has been a friend for more than 30 years and a business partner for more than 15. He was a talented executive and is a wonderful man. He has written a practical guide to investing that anyone from age 16 to 65 should read. He offers insights that are critical to smart investing and wealth creation that anyone can understand and put to work. He developed his approach to investing while teaching inmates in a federal prison about the basics of wealth creation. Investing is not just for rich people. Brad's approach is important for people who want to get rich, but slowly, patiently, and over a long period of time."

– Ted Jaroszewicz, Corporate CEO and Investor

"In the world of today, short term advice and instant gratification are the norm due to the explosion of social media and internet usage. The unrealistic images of instant wealth and everyone quickly profiting from the latest fad is not accurate given the reality of the fundamental path to successful investing. Through this book, Brad has reminded investors about the tried and true methods to begin to create wealth and get yourself on a course to success in all types of markets. This is a great tool for a whole new generation of investors to secure a wealth building future that is durable and understandable."

– Mark Lehmann, President, JMP Securities

"*The Roadside Scholar* is a must-read for adults young and old. Brad Stinn has distilled the often mystifying world of personal finance into a readable, practical guide for people to begin investing immediately. He maps a journey for young adults to participate in wealth-creation mechanism available to all. *The Roadside Scholar* makes a great high school graduation gift."

– Joe Vollert, Vice President of Advancement, Saint Ignatius College Preparatory

"My entire career has been focused on telling stories in a way that touches people. The story of *The Roadside Scholar* will do just that. It has a beautiful beginning, a tragic middle and then a triumphant return. It tackles an important topic in a way that surprises and the message to understand and focus on money matters rings true. Brad makes personal finance come to life— who knew the topic could be so entertaining. Well done."

– William M. Campbell III, TV Executive

THE
ROADSIDE
SCHOLAR

AMAZING **MONEY LESSONS**
FROM BEHIND THE FENCE

BRAD STINN

Cover design by N. Baburski

Library of Congress Catalog Card No. 7801374831

ISBN 978-0-578-53372-8

Printed in the United States of America

First Printing: July 2019

For ordering information, information about special discounts for bulk purchases or to arrange a speaking engagement please contact The Roadside Scholar, Inc.

Published by The Roadside Scholar, Inc.
P.O. Box 63
6 Beach Road
Tiburon, CA 94920
www.theroadsidescholar.com

Contents

The Roadside Scholar i

Preface v

Introduction ix

Part I: Do Not Make a Plan 1

Part II: Happiness is Positive Cash Flow 15

Part III: Do Not Save 45

    Stocks 55

    Bonds 91

Part IV: Be an Owner 121

Part V: Never Sell 173

Epilogue 211

Acknowledgements 214

Appendices 217

    Appendix A: Stinn Case Summary 218

    Appendix B: Double Double 222

    Appendix C: Company Valuation Ratios 224

    Appendix D: Glossary 227

Bibliography 234

To Jill, Sarah, Jack and Nick, without your love and positive attitudes, I would have given up years ago.

The Roadside Scholar

In prison, everyone gets a nickname. Years ago when I first began teaching business classes to inmates, a young guy, "Indian Joe" we called him, came up to me in our housing unit to ask a question. By way of background, "Indian Joe" was constantly in trouble, always brawling and spending significant time in the disciplinary unit. He asked, "Are you the guy teaching the new business class?" I answered in the affirmative. He then asked, "Is it true that you went to Harvard?" Again, I answered in the affirmative. He tilted his head to the side, gave me a skeptical up and down look, and asked with a quizzical expression, "Does that mean you are some kind of Roadside Scholar?" I answered without hesitation, "Yes, I think it does." From then on, I was The Roadside Scholar.

Yes, you read correctly. The author of this book, The Roadside Scholar, was a Federal inmate.

I went to prison in 2009 after being convicted of securities fraud. I had been the Chief Executive Officer of a public company that Federal prosecutors accused of disclosure violations in documents filed with the Securities and Exchange Commission. The prosecutors felt that the company had not adequately described certain of its accounting and business practices to the investing public. At trial they stated that while such practices were not out of compliance with regulations, the inaccurate disclosures harmed the investing public. As the CEO who signed the documents, I was held criminally liable despite the fact that I was the largest individual shareholder and had not sold a single share in my entire 11-year tenure as CEO. (For additional legal background refer to Appendix A.)

Federal prison in its simplest terms is a people warehouse: think big, sprawling Amazon facility with boxes stacked high. In this case, the boxes are human beings. Bodies are given a stock keeping number, jammed together on a shelf collecting dust and forgotten about by the outside world for years.

Prison was an alien environment. My only knowledge of it came from television and movies. I did not know what to expect and was scared stiff. One of the first things that happens to the new inmate is referred to as "checking paperwork," a process of examining the new guy's sentencing report to confirm that he is not a government informant or sex offender. When my cellmates read that I was convicted of scooping (what the prosecutors' called one of our accounting practices), they laughed. One guy in particular, a career marijuana smuggler, could not stop repeating the word scooping in a stilted voice and calling me the only criminal scooper he had ever met. Amazingly, the scooping label helped me fit in and eased my transition.

The biggest challenge I faced as an inmate was to stay engaged in productive activities. I responded to this challenge by teaching investment and business classes. I have a Harvard economics degree, and had been a financial analyst for a major Wall Street firm and the CEO of a publicly traded company for more than a decade. My experience and training enabled me to make a positive contribution to our community through teaching.

Teaching in prison is tough because the guys detest phonies and have a hard time focusing in the classroom. To have credibility, a teacher must know the material cold and communicate it in a way that grabs and holds their attention. I made sure that every fact was backed up with multiple credible sources. Through nearly ten years of trial and error, I learned to teach in a more entertaining and effective way.

The teaching was gratifying. Many took the lessons to heart and began using the strategies while still incarcerated. Family members would open capital accounts and invest for them. They got on the wealth creation train and their re-entry to society was easier as a result. Many went out of their way to thank me, buying commissary items they knew I liked, writing emails to staff complimenting the classes or sending notes back from the outside world expressing gratitude.

Because of my recent circumstances, my wife is skeptical that anyone will bother to read this book. She has a valid point. Why would anyone take money advice from a felon?

Interestingly, my time in prison helps answer the question. Courtesy of the Federal Government, I had the time to read extensively and research with no opportunity cost. I did not have to put food on the table or pay the mortgage or other bills. I was well prepared for the job having the appropriate educational background and a finance career as training. Plus, I was able to practice with real students for years, trying new ideas and concepts and gauging their reactions. I learned what worked and what did not.

I would also tell the reader the same thing I tell students the first day of class. Every statement that I make can be supported by multiple, credible sources, which is why my classes and this book are full of data and statistics. I do not want anyone to take my word for anything. Examine the numbers and look at the sources. If at any point a reader has a question or a concept is not clear, send an email to **theroadsidescholar.com** and I will explain the reasoning for the statement and provide the information source.

The experience of teaching in prison gave me deep insight into what people want to know about money and investing but are never taught. My hope is that many will use the strategies described herein to meaningfully increase their financial strength and improve the quality of their lives.

Preface

"Before you can write anything, you have to notice something," observed American author John Irving.

I never thought I would write a book. In the process of teaching money-related topics in prison, however, I noticed something important and felt compelled to write.

The vast majority of Americans have been done a disservice by our educational system relating to money matters and investing. These subjects are not taught in most schools and, when they are, the focus is too often on how to borrow efficiently or properly manage credit cards. Rarely is the focus on creating a second stream of income and accumulating wealth.

The demise of company-sponsored pension plans in favor of 401(k) investment accounts puts even more responsibility on the individual to make sound financial decisions. It has never been more important for working Americans to learn something about managing money.

I noticed this glaring problem in a roundabout way. To stay busy and keep active, I began to teach investing, accounting and marketing classes. One day, I signed up to take a class taught by an inmate titled, "Financial Literacy." I took the class because I was curious as to what my fellow inmate considered financial literacy. The teacher was a friend, supremely charming and likable, and an awesome speaker. He immediately had the class of 35 in the palm of his hand. I was mesmerized by his presentation skills and appalled at the same time as about half of what he was teaching was wrong, in some cases dangerously wrong.

In his lectures, he harped on the fact that money concepts were not taught in public schools (implying that they were in private schools) as part of a conspiracy to keep people down economically. While I did not agree with his conspiracy perspective, it was true that basic, important financial knowledge is not being taught in most American schools, public or private.

For the next several days, this sad truth kept rolling around in my head, particularly as it related to my three teenage children and my fatherly responsibilities. Did their schools teach money matters? No. What had I done with my financial training to fill this gaping hole? Nothing.

Then it hit me. Here was a perfect way to stay connected with them despite our physical separation and teach critical life lessons as well. It was a non-threatening topic (read: not about homework or boyfriends/girlfriends) that could be discussed during our periodic visits and ten minute phone calls.

After this realization, I threw myself at the project with a vengeance, ordering money and investment books and poring over every page of *The Wall Street Journal, Barron's* and *USA Today* business section for information and research. I clipped articles, saving them in a folder for future reference since we lacked internet and computer access. In my classes, I started experimenting with how best to teach the concepts. I learned a lot by listening to the comments and questions of my students and children. In so doing, some important things became obvious.

Everyone wants to be financially strong, yet most have not been taught how to go about accomplishing this objective. Those that try are often intimidated by the confusing jargon, acronyms and mathematical formulas of the financial world, get discouraged and log out. The prospect of making a mistake and losing money terrifies most people. They conclude that financial freedom is beyond their capabilities. Inaction and lost opportunity is the result.

I noticed that my teenage children and their friends cannot comprehend a time when they would not be young and carefree. Getting them to focus on critically important but boring financial matters by referencing retirement planning is a complete waste of breath. They give the "Dad, I am so annoyed with you" eye roll and tune out. If, however, you pitch the ideas in terms of improving their lives now -- not 45 years from now -- then they will put down the iPhone and listen.

It became apparent that most people equate saving with investing. Parking money in a KeyBank savings account earning 0.4% per year is perceived to be prudent investing. The reality is that savings accounts should be renamed guaranteed losing accounts. They generally fail to pay interest sufficient to match the rate of price inflation: the saver becomes poorer each year. Conversely, the explicit goal of investing is to increase purchasing power by earning a profit that exceeds the rate of inflation. All too often after explaining the difference in class I would hear, "Why didn't someone tell me this when I was younger?"

It was crystal clear that more resources need to be devoted to teaching basic investing and money matters. Most Americans are dangerously uninformed. Moreover, more impactful ways of teaching money matters were desperately needed. When I first started teaching, I too used the jargon and acronyms thinking I was doing the right thing. Over time, I learned that students would understand better and retain more information if I labeled concepts with fun names or used memorable phrases. They would laugh and joke, but would be more engaged. Attendance was better and classes were more fun.

This book is the product of approximately ten years of research and trial and error searching for the best ways to teach money matters to my students and children. It is intended to be a step-by-step guide and a valuable resource for those interested in building financial strength and achieving financial freedom. My hope is that it is understandable, memorable and, most importantly, actionable.

My ultimate goal is to make it clear that anyone in the United States of America can achieve financial freedom regardless of age, gender, religion, race, or level of education. All it takes is a steadfast commitment to the process and strategies described in this book. The only fatal mistake is sitting on the sidelines.

In class, I tell a story which I ran across when reading Tony Robbins' book, *Money: Master the Game* about a man who prospered playing the wealth creation game. He was a UPS employee who never earned more than $14,000 a year, but set aside 20% of every paycheck and holiday bonus to buy UPS stock. The value of this man's investment grew to more than $70 million by the time he was 90 years old.

My students love this story. What they take away from it is, "If this guy can do it, then I can." They can and you can too.

Introduction

This book is organized around the advice that I teach in my classes and have given my children: the actions to take to create a second stream of income and build wealth. It is a user's guide to creating financial freedom and increasing choices at every stage of life.

Nearly every personal finance article or book begins with the advice to "make a plan" and then lists the zillion pieces of data needed to complete a comprehensive plan. In practice, most need a session or two with a patient financial advisor just to understand the questions to be answered.

When I started teaching, I too began with the advice to "make a plan." While technically accurate, I quickly learned that this conventional wisdom is bad real world advice because too often it leads to inaction. When the typical person hears "make a (financial) plan," they assume it is a complicated, time consuming process that only the financially sophisticated can complete. Some believe only already rich people make financial plans. As a result, they procrastinate and do nothing -- an extremely costly decision. The United States Department of Labor estimates that for every 10 years of delay, a person needs to save 3 times the amount to catch up.

Now my advice is radically different. It is: "Start. Start Now. Do Not Delay."

In Part I titled, **Do Not Make a Plan**, I discuss the mechanics of opening a "capital account" which acts as the foundation of a wealth creation program. It is a brokerage account with a reputable securities firm that enables the purchase and sale of the full range of investments.

Establishing this account costs nothing and takes about 15 minutes start to finish. The capital account is then used to make investments designed to build purchasing power. It is not a savings account for short-term needs, but rather a long-term investment vehicle. There are no valid reasons to avoid opening a capital account.

Unless you are fortunate to have the proverbial rich uncle, money must be deposited from your paycheck into the capital account. In Part II, **Happiness is Positive Cash Flow**, a way to assess your financial position is presented. The goal is to maximize the deposits into your capital account.

Positive cash flow is defined as having more money coming in from paychecks than going out in expenses on a monthly or yearly basis. Part II outlines strategies to maximize the income part of the equation as well as minimize and control the expense side of the formula. Concepts such as Goal Setting, Double Time, Measure to Manage, and Have It Your Way are introduced.

While conceptually straightforward, achieving positive cash flow requires personal discipline and can be difficult to achieve as the entire United States economy is designed to separate us from our money. We are bombarded every day with slick advertising messages selling the next great product or extolling the benefits derived from paying more for the premium brand. The better able one is to manage finances to a positive each month, the more capital will be available to build wealth.

Part III: **Do Not Save** begins with an explanation of the fundamental difference between saving and investing and makes the argument that investing for the long-term is the only way to create wealth. Admittedly, investing involves risk of loss and more price volatility than parking money in a KeyBank savings account. Historically, however, the substantially higher profits generated by longer term investments have more than compensated for the additional risk.

Importantly, the investment landscape has changed dramatically over the last 30 years with the creation of funds that allow the individual investor to access low cost, sophisticated, and diversified investment portfolios. There has never been a more advantageous time for the individual to build wealth.

The two major categories of investments, stocks and bonds, are described and explained in **Do Not Save**. Today, a dizzying array of investment choices exist that are derivatives of these two basic categories. The individual investor would be wise to ignore the more complex options and keep investments simple.

Do Not Save explains what the investor needs to know about a range of basic investing concepts and terms, including price inflation, investment profit and loss measurement, valuation, liquidity, diversification and volatility.

How are the prices of stocks and bonds that appear online or in the newspaper determined? What makes a stock price a bargain or a bad deal? My typical student and probably the average person when asked if a stock is cheap or expensive will answer relative to its per share stock price: higher is a bad deal, lower is a good deal. They are surprised and often skeptical when I explain how Warren Buffet's company, Berkshire Hathaway, selling for approximately $256,000 for one share is a significantly better bargain than the stock of Under Armour trading for approximately $21 per share.

Do Not Save is the longest section, filled with information, and may seem a bit tedious. Read it slowly and in digestible bites. Having a baseline understanding of major investing concepts is important. Understanding the nature of what one owns and its typical price fluctuations is critical to staying the course, particularly when the markets receive a shock that results in dramatic price swings. Use this section as a reference.

Perhaps the most important piece of advice I have to offer is to **Be an Owner**. In order to achieve wealth, one must invest in ownership assets and not settle for the lower returns derived from lending (purchasing government or corporate bonds) or saving.

The most persuasive way to communicate this argument is by looking at the numbers. The following table shows what $10,000 grows into if invested for 30 years at either the average annual historical return of the U.S. stock market or the current annual interest rate on the 30 year U.S. Government Bond (all interest and dividends are assumed to be reinvested).

	Annual Total Return	Ending Amount	Wealth Created in Excess of inflation
Stock Market	9.6%	$156,400	$137,200
30 Year Bond	3.0%	$24,300	$5,100
Inflation	2.2%	$19,200	

As the data show, owning the U.S. stock market has created the most wealth and purchasing power -- well over $100,000 more.

Part IV: **Be an Owner** describes how to create a diversified portfolio of stock investments with a high probability of success. The investor can get the annual return of the U.S. market (the "market return") or utilize other strategies that have performed better historically than the market benchmark.

Taking a small amount of time to understand these winning stock market strategies is worth the effort as even slight outperformance makes a substantial impact over long time periods. In Part IV, these strategies are described. I have found that attaching a fun label helps my students understand and better remember the concepts. Here you will find: **Smaller is Bigger, Pay Less, Get More, Go With the Mo** and **Bonus Bundles.**

If **Be an Owner** is the most important piece of advice in this book, Part V: **Never Sell** is the hardest to accomplish. **Never Sell** means that to get the maximum benefits of investing, one needs to invest for the long-term. Conceptually, this is easy, but as the markets gyrate up and down in a seemingly random manner, it is difficult to stay the course. Investing for the long-term involves delayed gratification and the strength to resist the natural tendency for short-term rewards.

In most personal finance courses, the benefit of this advice is delivered by explaining the magic, mathematical concept of compound interest. While I do explain compound interest in Part V, I have found that the phrase **Never Sell** is more impactful and direct. The rationale for **Never Sell** is straightforward: no one has proven the ability, after fees, trading costs and taxes, to be able to profitably time the markets on a consistent basis. Hence, the strategy of buying and holding a diversified portfolio will deliver higher profits to the investor.

The UPS employee that Tony Robbins described is an example of what can happen if one follows the advice in this book. He started. He managed his finances to positive cash flow, setting aside 20% of every paycheck to invest. He did not park the money in a savings account; he consistently bought stock. He was an owner of a great American business -- UPS. He held on for a long time and never sold, letting the magic of compound interest work.

If you apply the concepts in this book and have the personal discipline to stick with the program, you too can be fabulously successful.

Part I
Do Not Make a Plan

1

Start Now

Wealth and the financial freedom it creates is a choice available to all Americans. No laws or insurmountable obstacles stand in the way. The institutions of wealth creation in this country, including banks, securities firms and the stock and bond markets, are open and available to all, irrespective of age, race, gender, education or income level. In fact, the evolution of the capital markets in the U.S. over the last 50 years combined with the internet age have radically transformed investing. Today the individual investor can easily and cost efficiently acquire winning investments and manage a sophisticated portfolio.

Sadly, too few understand the opportunity and take advantage. Many fall prey to the poverty of expectations: people are not encouraged to believe they can build wealth, so most do not try. Yet, the fact is that any American with desire and personal discipline can become rich.

Once the decision has been made to get on the wealth formation train, conventional financial wisdom calls for the individual to "make a plan." A comprehensive plan would include outlining life goals and expected income levels; anticipating family size, educational needs, and health problems; making estimates of stock and bond market returns for the next 30 or 40 years or until retirement; and assessing risk tolerance. Just listing the plan inputs makes one dizzy. For most, it is a very intimidating task and involves too much guesswork.

"Making a plan" is a waste of time and effort. No one can accurately predict even one year into the future for any one of the factors listed above, much less for all of them for the next 30 or 40 years. Furthermore, if one has never made an investment, how can that person possibly be expected to make a sound and accurate judgment of risk tolerance? In the real world, the advice to "make a plan" usually leads to delay and procrastination which is expensive. Worse still, the inability to complete this step often leads to permanent inaction. Inaction means never getting on the path to wealth.

Consulting a financial advisor who can assist in creating a plan is an option. While this can make the process much easier, financial advisors do not have crystal balls to accurately predict the future either. Plus, a financial advisor's time dedicated to making the plan must be paid for in the form of a concurrent fee or a promise of future fees.

Another alternative is to study the fields of financial planning and investment in an attempt to become a proficient money manager. In fact, some very smart people recommend just this course of action. The following quote from one of my favorite books, *The Intelligent Asset Allocator* by William J. Bernstein, exemplifies this view.

"Take a deep breath, and do nothing for several weeks or months, or as long as it takes to complete the following steps (six steps are listed including gaining an understanding of the risk/reward relationship, understanding portfolio theory, and estimating your risk tolerance). You are in no rush to immediately and radically alter your finances. You have the rest of your life to get your affairs in order......"

This is poor advice. If creating wealth and increasing purchasing power improve one's life, then why should the individual not be in a rush to get started?

Making a serious mistake is a valid concern. However, the process involved in getting started is simpler than commonly perceived.

As a result, my advice is quite different. Do Not Delay. Do Not Make Excuses. Get Over Your Fear. Start Now.

Every day of inaction is wealth lost. Every day your money is parked in a savings account earning 0.4% annual interest while prices increase by 2% per year is making you poorer. Be in a rush to alter your finances for the better -- a thoughtful rush, but a rush nonetheless. Since time is an investor's best friend, wasting time is the most expensive decision an individual can make.

One day I was making this point in an Investing Class -- perhaps too energetically for an early morning group -- when a funny thing happened. One of the guys had taken a Marketing Class previously which as a group project had created a tagline for the Camp Education Department's communications with inmates -- "Don't Waste Your Crime. Do Smart Time." Everyone knew the line because it was plastered all over the Camp's classrooms and bulletin boards. Trying to get a reaction from his half-awake classmates, he blurted out, "The advertising line for this class should be -- "Don't Waste Time. It's a Crime." He got a big laugh and also perfectly captured the essence of the advice.

Start Now.

2

Capital Account

To get started, open what I refer to as a "capital account" with a reputable brokerage firm.

To explain the objective of a capital account begin with a review of the word capital itself. According to *Merriam-Webster's Collegiate Dictionary*, the word capital has a number of definitions depending on its usage and context. One definition is "chief in importance." When used in an exclamation like, "What a capital idea!", it means an excellent or important idea. When used in the context of money another meaning is "accumulated goods devoted to the production of income." Words whose meanings are identical or nearly identical include advantage, resources, net worth and wealth.

I take literary license with these definitions by combining them to emphasize and explain the importance of getting into the capital formation game.

My hybrid description of capital is: It is an excellent idea to accumulate goods devoted to the production of income. With capital, one gains advantage and increases net worth and wealth.

A capital account in practical terms is a relationship with a reputable securities firm devoted to the production of wealth for the account owner. The relationship may consist of one or more accounts which together facilitate the cost efficient purchase and sale of stocks and bonds on all major national and international exchanges. A relationship with a reputable firm is required as a trustworthy custodian to securely hold the owner's resources is a necessity. A capital account is long-term in nature and is not intended to be used to pay for current expenses.

BROKERAGE FIRMS

Securities brokerage firms can be sorted in to two major categories: full service and discount or online firms. Increasingly, the line between the two is narrowing as many firms are offering both full service and discount alternatives to their customers. Both types of firms offer trading execution (buying and selling), market research, margin loans, monthly and annual statements and cash management alternatives. The major distinction between full service and online firms is the level of individual service provided to the customer.

In the case of a full service firm, one account representative, commonly referred to as a broker, is assigned to an individual's account. The broker handles the paperwork associated with opening the account. That representative works with the customer to understand his or her financial objectives and needs, and to design a suitable investment plan. The broker then executes the plan and keeps the client informed as to the status of the account and any recommended changes. Merrill Lynch, Morgan Stanley, Goldman Sachs, Wells Fargo, Raymond James and Edward Jones are examples of reputable, full service securities brokerage firms. Many of these firms require minimum dollar amounts to open an account.

Historically, full service brokers were paid based on commissions generated from trading stocks and bonds. In recent years, the compensation model has evolved so that most firms offer the client the option of a commission-based payment plan or an annual fee plan where the amount paid is calculated as a percentage of the dollar amount of the account.

For online brokerage firms, the individual initiates contact and opens the account either by visiting the firm's web site or walking into an investor relations center. While this involves more effort and time than opening an account with a full service firm, all the large online firms have excellent, easy to navigate web sites and 24-hour telephone support to make the paperwork process go smoothly and quickly.

Online firms do not dedicate a representative to each client to create an investment plan and make trades. The client is required to decide what stocks, bonds and funds to purchase and to enter the trades into the computer. This is referred to as a self-directed investment program.

Once the account is established, the client is able to make trades up to the level of cash available in the account. Online brokers typically earn a flat fee per trade executed, currently ranging from $4.95 to $7.99 per trade. The most prominent online brokers are Fidelity, Charles Schwab, TD Ameritrade, E*Trade, Interactive Brokers and Vanguard.

The principal difference between full service and online brokers is the level of personalized investment advice offered to the client. In a full service arrangement, the broker is expected to offer expert financial advice and trade execution. Because service levels are higher, a relationship with a full service brokerage firm is more expensive for the investor. Unless annual investment profits are commensurately higher, this can be a bad deal for the client.

ACCOUNT TYPES

With either type of broker, an investor has the option of opening a taxable account, referred to as a regular brokerage account, or a tax-advantaged account such as an Individual Retirement Account ("IRA") or both. In a regular brokerage account, all deposits into the account are made with after-tax dollars and all investment gains and losses on securities held are subject to Federal and State income tax annually. Tax-advantaged accounts are designed to comply with certain incentives built into the tax code in order to encourage saving for retirement or for college educational expenses. Examples of such tax-advantaged accounts are employer-sponsored 401(k) plans, traditional and Roth individual retirement accounts ("IRAs"), and 529 plan (education) accounts. The dollar benefit to using these types of accounts are substantial.

For example, contributions to a Traditional IRA are tax deductible if made from earned income and currently can total $6,000 per year. Additionally, investment gains in a Traditional IRA are not subject to annual income tax. Investors pay tax only when amounts are withdrawn from a Traditional IRA at the individual's income tax rate then in effect. An important restriction on a Traditional IRA is a 10% penalty incurred for withdrawals before the account holder reaches age 59 1/2.

The benefits of participating in a Traditional IRA are substantial. First, the investor realizes a reduction in current period taxes, as shown below.

Contribution to Traditional IRA: $6,000	
Tax Reduction at Tax Rate of:	
25%	$1,500
30%	$1,800
35%	$2,100

Second, the investor will profit from future investment gains on the taxes foregone, as shown below.

Initial Taxes Saved	Balance @ 9% for 30 Years	Taxes at Withdrawal	Total Profit from Deferral
$1,500	$19,900	25%: $4,975	$14,925
$1,800	$23,900	30%: $7,170	$16,730
$2,100	$27,900	35%: $9,765	$18,135

Generally, individuals should maximize contributions to tax-advantaged accounts.

IMPORTANCE OF MINIMIZING BROKERAGE FEES

It is important to realize that profits from investing are reduced by fees and commissions paid to brokerage firms and money managers. The wise investor seeks to minimize these expenses as seemingly small amounts can add up to large dollars over time.

The table below highlights the impact of various fee levels.

Annual Investment Gain:	9%	
$10,000 Becomes (30 years)	$132,700	
Amount After Annual Fees of:		
0.5%	$115,600	Decrease of 13%
1.0%	$100,600	Decrease of 24%

As the above data shows, the investor loses between 13% and 24% of his total dollars by paying annual fees of 0.5% to 1.0%.

The investor should expect to incur some amount of trading and management fees for maintaining a capital account. However, a prudent investor is aware of fees being charged and seeks to minimize the amount in order to maximize his profit as opposed to the broker's profit.

3

Open an Account Now

Get Started. Finish this chapter and then put the book down, log on to an online broker's web site and open a capital account. Be in a rush to get on the wealth creation train.

I recommend going with the online brokerage option. Today, the small investor can assemble a winning diversified portfolio without paying the higher fees associated with full service brokers. Even though great financial advisors are worth the fees they charge, there are too few great ones and too many poor ones. The investor just getting started with a small dollar amount to invest will not be a priority for the super broker. With a subpar broker, expect bad financial advice and increased pressure to trade, resulting in underperformance.

The online brokerage option is also the low cost option. Even small fee savings every year add up to large additional dollars in your account down the road.

Among online brokers, I recommend Fidelity or Charles Schwab. Both are outstanding choices for the small investor as transaction fees are low, trade execution for small orders is excellent, and they provide the full array of other services such as portfolio reporting, individual securities and fund research and trading analysis. Importantly, Fidelity and Schwab, as two of the country's largest investment firms, are highly reputable and stable, have excellent account security, and have easy to use web sites with friendly and helpful 24-hour phone support.

Fidelity is highly ranked among online brokerage houses: *Barron's* ranked Fidelity number one in 2016 and 2017; *Investor's Business Daily* named Fidelity the Top Online Brokerage Firm in 2015, 2016 and 2017; and *Kiplinger's* magazine in 2016 said Fidelity was a 5 time winner of the title of Best Overall Online Broker.

Among online brokers, *J. D. Power* ranked Charles Schwab number one and Fidelity number two.

If you already have a brokerage relationship, ask your broker for an analysis of the annual investment profits for your account for the last 5 years compared to an appropriate market benchmark and for a schedule of fees and commissions you paid, expressed in both dollar terms and as a percentage of the total account balance per year. Review these schedules to see how well your gross investment returns compared to the benchmark and how fees and commissions paid affected your returns. If you are lucky enough to have a great broker, stay with your existing program. If your returns are low and fees are high, make a change.

If you are working full time and expect to deposit $6,000 or less in the next year, open a Traditional IRA. Over time, contributing the maximum to a tax-advantaged account puts tens of thousands of extra dollars in your pocket rather than in federal and state tax coffers. Also, take advantage of employer sponsored 401(k) plans especially if the company matches contributions. Check with a tax professional to make sure you do not exceed the combined annual limits on these types of programs.

If you are planning to invest amounts beyond the combined annual limits of an IRA and a 401(k) plan, then also open a regular brokerage account.

If you are opening an account for a minor or a full time student, then opt for the regular brokerage account as tax-advantaged accounts are not applicable.

Deposit money into your account(s) as soon and as often as possible.

After initiating the appropriate brokerage relationship, come back to this book and continue reading. Look to the remaining chapters for advice on maximizing personal cash flow and strategies for creating winning, cost and tax efficient portfolios.

Part II

Happiness is Positive Cash Flow

1

Buy a Pillow

Happiness is positive cash flow. In the early days of my marriage when cash was scarce, I repeated this maxim seemingly daily to my beautiful, young bride. After a while, she grew so weary of hearing it that she bought me a pillow embroidered with the phrase for my birthday.

I love the adage (and the pillow) because it summarizes a fundamental truth of personal and corporate finance. Having more money coming in than going out brings peace of mind, including marital harmony, and creates a cash surplus that can be allocated to investing and wealth creation. Conversely, failure to achieve positive cash flow creates extreme tension for individuals and companies -- bills piling up, annoying phone calls from creditors, the necessity of borrowing money and, often, nasty arguments between partners.

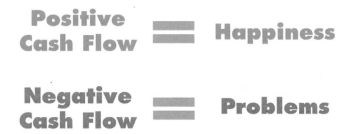

Positive cash flow for the individual is defined as having more money coming in from the paycheck than being spent on expenses. Conceptually, attaining positive cash flow is a snap. In practice, it can be much more elusive.

Many wrongly view the income half of the equation as a finite amount, a limit, instead of something that can be managed and increased. The commonly repeated phrase "live within your means" reinforces the limit mind-set. It suggests not to dream or even think about how to increase your income stream. Nor does it hint at the idea of creating a second stream of income from investments.

The subliminal message being delivered is "know your place and stay in it." While it is true that it is wise to regularly spend less than one makes, the individual would be well served to think about income differently, not as a finite amount but rather as a starting point.

Even more damaging to your financial health is the fact that American companies spend billions and billions each year on marketing and advertising trying to part us from our money. Every minute of every day TV and radio commercials, internet advertisements, roadside billboards, and print advertisements are pitching new products or reinforcing the brand identities of existing products. Worse still are the slick, aspirational messages urging us to crave and buy the premium product -- the expensive Mercedes sedan versus a comparably sized Ford product at half the cost, for example.

To hammer this point home in Money Smart class, I ask the inmate students to make a list of every product brand name they come across in a typical day. Even in prison the list is staggering. Colgate, Oral-B, Dove, Q-Tip, Suave, Speed Stick, Hanes, Fruit of the Loom, Russell Athletic, and Nike make the list just getting cleaned up and dressed in the morning. Try this exercise for one full day and you will be shocked.

Spending money is enjoyable and fun. Research studies have shown that shopping and spending is pleasurable and a form of entertainment for many; so enjoyable that some feel physical pleasure similar to the exercise induced runner's high. Making matters more treacherous, shopping has never been easier and faster than it is today with 24 hour internet access and one click purchasing options.

If wealth creation is the goal, then positive cash flow is a requirement because a monthly surplus fuels the engine of wealth creation, the capital account.

2

Set a Goal

The key to positive cash flow is to take charge of your money. Do not think of your income as a fixed amount and do not let expenses just happen.

Establish precise short-term targets and less precise, more directional long-term objectives.

Set a specific and realistic, but aggressive, monthly goal. Do it now and write it down. Aim for a percentage of net pay after taxes or a fixed dollar amount. Do not employ a vague goal such as "save as much as possible." No one can successfully manage to such an objective.

Think positively and expansively. Managing to a target is not a limit concept. What do you want to achieve? What are your dreams?

Language matters. Never use the word budget because it carries a negative connotation, implying only spending cuts and fun reduction. Rather think of yourself as a business seeking to make a monthly profit and increase that profit as rapidly as possible. You are the CEO of your life and need to manage to the intended result. Open your mind to new income opportunities. Think about each expense and establish a spending hierarchy. Decide which expenditures matter to you and which do not. Make managing to positive cash flow a challenge, an adventure, a game.

DOUBLE TIME

One easy and fun way to set a specific monthly cash flow goal is to play what I call Double Time. My Investing and Money Smart students complete this exercise and have fun with it as doubling one's money is always an exciting topic. Doing the calculations in class makes the path to the double understandable and real.

In Double Time, each student is asked how quickly they would like to double the amount of money in their investment account. Then, using the mathematical Rule of 72, they calculate what needs to happen to double the balance.

To play Double Time, divide 72 by the number of years the individual wishes to double his or her funds. For example, if one wants to double in 6 years, an annual contribution equal to 12% of the beginning balance is required. Each year for 6 years, 12% of the beginning balance must be deposited. Note that as the balance grows, each subsequent year requires a greater contribution.

DOUBLE TIME

72 ÷ Years to DOUBLE = % to Save Each Year

DOUBLE TIME

72 ÷ % Saving Per Year = Years to DOUBLE Money

DOUBLE TIME EXAMPLE

Beginning Balance:	$3,000
Double Time Goal:	6 years
Deposit Required:	12% Per Year

Year	Amount Required
1	$360/$30 per month
2	$403/$34 per month
3	$452/$38 per month
4	$506/$42 per month
5	$567/$47 per month
6	$634/$53 per month

In class, the students change the assumptions to fit their own circumstances and objectives and calculate realistic individual goals. The reaction is always the same: First, an incredulous, "Is that all I have to save?" and then "I can do that."

After playing Double Time for a bit, the students realize that as the beginning account balance increases a short Double Time of 3 or 4 years becomes more difficult because the amount of required deposits often increases past the point of realism. With a large beginning balance, a longer Double Time of 5 or 6 years may be more realistic. The great thing about Double Time is that precise achievable goals can be set whatever the dollar starting point.

Refer to Appendix B for Double Double, an advanced version of Double Time incorporating both the savings rate and a portfolio's expected investment rate.

Before going further, calculate what you need to save each month to double your money.

MEASURE TO MANAGE

Essential to mastering the process of achieving positive cash flow is understanding that everything can be measured and that only by measuring something can it be managed. Simply quantifying a dollar amount that you want to increase your income by makes the task of finding that extra income easier. Collecting and categorizing monthly expenditures, quantifying the cost of alternatives and placing them side by side, makes decision-making faster, less nerve-racking and better.

POSITIVE CASH FLOW

Managing finances so that inflows exceed required outflows is the definition of positive cash flow. When this happens, a cash surplus is created that can be allocated to emergency cash reserves or invested in the capital account to increase net worth. The math is straightforward: Monthly After-Tax Income minus Required Expenditures equals Profit or Positive Cash Flow.

CASH FLOW
$Income$ — Expenses = + or – Cash Flow

Each element of the equation deserves focus. How can income be increased? How can expenses be reduced while maintaining or even increasing quality of life?

3

Get Money Rolling In

There are two parts to the cash flow equation: income and expense. Why is 50% of the equation routinely ignored?

I have read *The Wall Street Journal, Barron's* and *USA Today* cover to cover for years while incarcerated and have clipped out and saved articles on personal finance from these and other publications such as *Forbes* and *Kiplinger's.* Before writing this section, I referenced my bulging file looking for articles that discuss strategies for increasing income. Amazingly, I could not locate even one. The best I could do was a reference in a publication that the Bureau of Prisons provides for use in the Money Smart class titled, *Financial Empowerment Curriculum: Moving Ahead Through Financial Management.* It says:

"If you do not have enough money to cover all the expenses, consider the following:

    -- Work a few extra hours at work.

    -- Avoid eating out at restaurants.

    -- Limit treats for your children."

This is poor advice. Only one of the three suggestions is even an income generating idea and a pretty lame one at that. Two relate to reducing expenses, including one that suggests that a great revenue strategy is to deny your children treats. With advice like that, it is no wonder people view personal financial management in a negative light.

In ignoring half the equation, the implication is that everyone already maximizes their income potential. Common sense argues against this conclusion.

Individuals must have a revenue strategy just like a corporate CEO must have an articulated growth strategy. The great news about developing an income growth mindset is that it is a positive emotion and energizing. It is certainly a lot more fun to take the initiative and think about how to bring home an extra $200-$500 per month than it is to see the look on your children's faces when denied treats.

INCOME GROWTH

Take responsibility for your annual income and its growth trajectory. Do not sit back and assume that you will be fairly compensated, earning what you deserve from your employer. Understand that it is the individual's responsibility to maximize income, not the employer's. Take action to make increases happen.

In the corporate world, the CEO's objective is to increase profits on behalf of shareholders. The CEO understands that revenue growth is essential to profit growth as expense management and cost cutting are only effective to a point: revenue increases are necessary to offset the constant pressure of rising costs and the need for reinvestment in the business.

Similarly, it is essential that the individual think proactively about income and not leave increases to chance. Individuals encounter the same inexorable year-over-year upward pressure on the prices of goods and services and have a need to fund a financial safety net. Moreover, even if cash flow is positive today, the individual's future income must rise faster than prices in order to maintain a positive result.

INCOME GROWTH IDEAS

Decide on the desired increase. Is the goal an additional few hundred dollars a month or is the goal much larger? Establishing this parameter is fundamental to identifying potential solutions.

In either case, it is a good idea to complete a personal professional inventory to understand your market value. Based on education, experience and current position, are you compensated above or below peers within your current company? How do you compare to others in similar positions at other companies? How competitive is your company in its industry and how fast is that industry growing? What is the demand for your skill set? How hard and expensive would it be for your employer to replace you?

Simply put -- know what you are worth. Establishing a realistic sense of your value in the marketplace increases the likelihood of successfully navigating to a permanently higher income level.

Current Employer

If the goal is a few hundred dollars more per month and you are happy in your job, then the easiest place to find more income is with your current employer. After completing the professional inventory, meet with your boss and discuss your desire for an increased pay packet. This discussion should be constructive, non-confrontational and non-emotional. Lay out your request and your rationale for it. Feel free to share your analysis. The work you put in to prepare for this discussion will show seriousness on your part and provide the facts to sell the request.

Make sure to be clear in the ask -- a raise of a certain dollar amount, a certain dollar per hour increase, more over time, a monthly incentive program based on quantifiable production metrics, or an annual bonus. If you have gauged your market value accurately, this process should result in an increase of some sort.

Part-Time Work

If an increase from your current employer is not feasible, then consider participating in a part-time, flexible work schedule job or traditional part-time employment.

Many flexible schedule, part-time job options are available today in our so called "gig" economy.

For example, my son and nephew, both college students, occasionally drive for Uber when they need extra cash and have free time. My nephew recently drove on the Saturday of the Ohio State University graduation weekend and earned $1,000 in fares and tips from happy parents of graduating seniors. My niece, a young professional, loves dogs but is too busy and travels too often to keep a pet. To satisfy her canine craving, she walks dogs when time allows for a service called Wag. One recent Saturday morning, she made $80 for a little over an hour doing something she enjoys. Another niece is an excellent artist and finds that the creative process relaxes her. She has advertised her talents on the internet and in her spare time creates beautiful line drawings for people.

The available universe of conventional part-time jobs with regular, set schedules is also expanding in the US economy, primarily because the traditional source of part-time workers, young adults, are increasingly forgoing such part-time work to pursue other interests.

Furthermore, as medical insurance costs skyrocket, employers are shifting more job functions to permanent part-time status -- which do not include medical care coverage and other employee benefits -- away from higher cost full time positions.

The best part-time jobs are ones that you enjoy performing the underlying work. If a wine connoisseur, seek a part-time job at a retail wine store. If a lover of fashion, try to find part-time work at a clothing boutique or representing a clothing line. If addicted to coffee, then pursue a weekend job at a coffee shop receiving not only the additional paycheck but also free coffee, thereby reducing the expense of your coffee habit. If in possession of bookkeeping or accounting skills, consider moonlighting for small, locally owned businesses.

A myriad of ways exist to pick up extra income, often times performing enjoyable activities. This is particularly true for the young adult with a more flexible schedule. Think expansively about your interests and skill set and look for something to do for a few hours per week that you enjoy.

Change Jobs or Careers

If seeking a significant increase in compensation or unhappy with your current job, consider making a change.

If fairly compensated for your professional experience and current education level, then perhaps additional education is the answer in a bid to elevate your earning power. High school graduates typically make more than workers without high school degrees. College graduates typically make more than high school graduates. Graduate degree holders usually have more career options than college graduates. Also, acquiring professional certifications and additional licenses can lead to increased pay (some employers pay for such training).

Do not commit to a new, costly education program blindly. A hard-nosed analysis must be completed comparing the cost of the additional education versus the probability of putting yourself on a permanently higher income plane. Be careful not to underestimate the payback time frame of additional education or vocational training as the average US worker is living and working longer, magnifying the return on an investment in education.

If not fairly compensated, begin a search for a new employer. If your personal professional inventory is an accurate assessment of the marketplace, then this process should yield a higher paying, more rewarding job.

Start a New Business

Consider starting a new business. Starting and owning your own business can be highly rewarding emotionally and financially.

The most commonly cited reasons why entrepreneurs start new enterprises are the excitement of the business challenge, the desire for a meaningful professional accomplishment, the desire for increased control over time and income, and the opportunity for a significant wealth creating event.

The successful entrepreneur typically possesses leadership skills in abundance, understands the relevant industry, has a vision of the company to be created, and is adept at communicating that vision to prospective employees, customers and investors.

Importantly, the successful entrepreneur exhibits emotional grit -- personal qualities such as discipline, dedication and persistence.

The downsides to starting and managing a new business are the never ending 24/7 work schedule, the sometimes overwhelming challenge to intellect and physical stamina, and the uncertainty of the outcome -- failure happens frequently. Not everyone is built for such a demanding assignment with no guarantee of success.

Entrepreneurship is one of the business classes that I have taught on several occasions during my years of incarceration. Surprisingly, it is one of the most popular classes as quite a few of my fellow inmates are interested in starting their own businesses upon release. In fact, the TV show, *Shark Tank*, is one of the most popular and watched shows in Federal prison.

One of the first topics we discuss in class is how to develop a new business concept. Most think that it involves drinking a magical potion, praying for divine inspiration or being hit by a thunderbolt out of the blue and are pleasantly surprised when the reality is more prosaic. In the real world, new business ideas are born out of business experience, experience as a customer, scientific research or as a result of a founder's hobbies and skills.

To come up with an idea, be curious and challenge conventional wisdom and the status quo. Start asking questions. What am I an expert in? Are there opportunities in my industry that my company and other companies are ignoring? Are there cost inefficiencies that I know how to address? Do I have a hobby that I can turn into a money making venture?

Do not fret if an idea does not immediately come to mind. Create the objective in your subconscious mind -- plant the seed -- and go about the day with a curious mind, open to possibilities. Eventually, the "aha" moment will happen and the beginnings of an idea for a new business will emerge.

I have experienced the thrill of the "aha" moment. In the spring of our freshman year at Harvard, two friends and I decided that we wanted to start a business to make some spending money -- nothing more specific. The only requirement was that the business had to be able to be performed around our class and football team schedule.

That summer, I went home to Ohio and ran into my grade school basketball coach who was in the carpet distribution business. He asked if I needed a rug for my dorm room for the following year and offered that they always had seconds and remnants available at attractive prices. I answered in the affirmative and then the "aha" moment hit: not only did I need a rug to cover the cold wood floors in the drafty, old Harvard dormitories, but many of my fellow students did as well. I immediately called my partners, floated the idea and our little venture, GQ Carpets, was born. GQ Carpets operated successfully through senior year, funding much of our activities.

WARNING: Approximately 50% of new business ventures fail in the first year of operation. Do not open a new business unless 100% committed. To increase the odds of success, develop a comprehensive business plan and confirm possession of a burning motivation to succeed. Hope for good luck.

4

Control Expenses

The second half of the Cash Flow Equation is the expense side of the ledger. The key to successfully managing expenses, balancing the desire to enjoy life while building wealth, can be distilled in one word -- control. The individual must be in control of his money and not allow other forces to rule the wallet, not the savvy ad men on Madison Avenue, not the iconic premium brands, not peer pressure and not friends or family. Just as your boss is not responsible for maximizing your income, no one else but you is responsible for spending your money.

Taking control is a straightforward three step process that takes minimal effort and a small amount of time. The only math expertise required is the ability to add, subtract, and multiply. The benefits far out weigh the effort expended. Yet, a surprisingly small percentage of the population make the effort to exert control over spending.

The first step of the three step process is to gather information and create a system of management. The next step is to think about psychology. What motivates you? What are your priorities? What typical stumbling blocks will you encounter? The last part is the fun part, the taking control step -- prioritizing expenditures consistent with long-term objectives and short-term goals and seeking better alternatives.

DO NOT BUDGET

Before getting to the specifics of the process, the word budget must be dealt with.

I have always perceived the word budget in a positive light. Every company I have ever been associated with managed to an annual budget. Growing up, my parents talked about managing money prudently and I assumed that they had a household budget. In my mind, having a budget meant that one was fiscally responsible.

When I started teaching Money Smart, I was surprised to learn that most students viewed the word budget negatively. What was particularly interesting is that it was not easy to get them to ad-mit to this fact. It was a feeling no one wanted to own up to in front of peers, especially in a class called Money Smart, almost as if it was a politically incorrect thought. At first, the majority would say that the word budget was a positive. Once pushed a little harder, they would admit that budgets were for people who "could not control themselves" or for people who "were not do-ing too good" or that budgets were "forced" on people.

To get this discussion going in class, I would ask the students a series of questions. What word pops into your head when you hear the word budget? The most common answer was "money" - - neither positive or negative, a neutral word. What other words come to mind? The most common answers were "bills," "cutting back," "broke," and "spend less." One guy said, "I don't have a budget. I'm a baller." When asked to explain why someone is on a budget, the most common answer approximates, "they are not doing very good." I would ask them to compare budgeting to an-other common, every day experience. One day a guy summed up the consensus feeling of the class saying, "It is like going to the dentist for a root canal."

When the word that is most commonly used to describe taking control of your financial life is viewed with disdain, as bad as going for a root canal, then another word or phrase is needed. Trying to change the negative perception of "budget" already in the mind of the typical person is a waste.

Now in class, we talk about "taking control" of expenses, completely omitting from our vocabulary the words budget or budgeting. Because the phrase "taking control" is perceived positively and creates a more empowering mind-set, people respond more favorably. Taking control is a choice, unlike budgeting which is forced upon someone.

Do not budget. Take control of your financial life.

STEP I: GATHER INFORMATION

Having accurate information is the first step to achieving control. Before beginning, know that most people underestimate their expenses and, as a result, overestimate their actual or potential savings. Do not assume and do not make judgments at this stage. Quantify. Collect the information necessary to establish an accurate spending profile.

Create a simple, easy to use system to collect data. Whether manual or automated, the system that feels the most comfortable to the user and leads to immediate action should be employed. Like many aspects of money management, the biggest mistake people make is procrastination. Never forget that lost time is lost money -- your money. Start getting the facts now.

The system can be as simple as a pencil and a piece of paper with receipts attached and daily cash outflows listed. It can be the old style accordion file with compartments to deposit receipts, organized by day of the month or by category. In class, a surprising number of the guys mention the envelope system whereby each category of expense has its own envelope for receipts to be placed.

Of course, laptop computers, smartphones and credit cards with links to electronic payment systems have automated many of these processes, making data collection happen automatically. "Taking Control" apps with names such as EarnUp, Digit, Qapital, and Simple strive to make the process easier and faster. Interestingly, a couple of these apps modify and automate the old fashioned envelope system. Also providing assistance are commercial banks and credit card companies which generally offer customers a historical month-by-month listing of payments and withdrawals.

Once the raw data are collected, the next step is to sort by category -- what the expenditure is for -- with notations for how often the bill is paid (frequency) and its contractual nature (fixed versus variable). The table below is an example presentation of this information.

Category	Definition	Frequency	Fixed/ Variable	Amount

Housing: All housing related expenses such as rent or mortgage payment, rental or mortgage related insurance, property taxes, utilities, gas, water, security alarm fees, etc.

Food: Grocery expenditures, the cost of meals eaten away from home, bottled water purchases, coffee purchases, and every item consumed.

Clothing: Expenses for clothing, shoes, etc.

Transportation: All automobile related expenses including car payment, insurance, gas, and maintenance. Also include any other regular transportation costs such as commuting expenses.

Family (if applicable): School tuition and fees, toys and the costs of extracurricular activities.

Phone: Home and mobile.

Insurance: Non-real estate and auto insurance, such as medical, life, and disability.

Loan Payments: Exclude mortgage and auto loan payments, includes student loan, credit card, retail store credit and other loans.

Entertainment: Movie and concert tickets, health club and golf club memberships, sports tickets, etc.

Other: Expenses not in one of the above categories.

Once all the information is loaded into the worksheet, add up the expenses and subtract the total from monthly income. Hopefully, the net number is positive from the start and the task is to optimize the result. If not, then the cost side of the equation needs focus.

STEP II: KNOW YOURSELF

Put all this information aside, sit back and relax for a moment. You have earned it. Just by assembling the information you are already more fiscally responsible than most.

Now it is time to understand how human nature and society erect roadblocks to good financial decision making. Getting these psychological biases working in your favor or, at a minimum, not against you is the secret to success.

<u>Psychological Roadblocks</u>

Perception of Control: The majority of the population has not stopped to think seriously about spending. Most opt to go with the flow of societal pressure, family tradition or other influencing forces, managing to get by each month but never getting ahead. Yet, if asked, most would say they were 100% in control of spending, significantly underestimating the extent to which outside stimuli sway decision making.

For example, family traditions are often accepted without question. To illustrate this point in class, I use the example of toothpaste. Each student is asked to declare their brand of choice; most often they are either a "Crest person" or a "Colgate person." Interestingly, about 90% of the guys use the same brand of toothpaste as adults that they (or their spouse) grew up using as children. I ask if anyone had made a conscious toothpaste brand decision. Almost to a person they say "no." When asked if Crest and Colgate are superior to other brands or each other, and if less expensive alternatives are just as good at cleaning teeth, no one has an answer.

I then pull out our commissary (inmate store) menu, which lists the items inmates can purchase weekly. Two different types of

Colgate are listed, one for $3.80 and another for $3.00 per tube. Even though they look at the list 52 times per year, when I point out that Close-Up, located just below Colgate, is priced at only $1.80 per tube, most are surprised.

Have they made a conscious decision that Colgate is superior to Close-Up and worth the extra money? No. They have been conditioned to prefer the stronger brand, not necessarily the better economic deal, and have not actively looked for alternatives. Admittedly, toothpaste is an inexpensive item -- saving $1.20 per tube will not make one wealthy. However, this type of bias applies to more expensive goods and services and saving 40% (e.g. $1.20 off $3.00 per tube) on every expense category would certainly make one prosperous.

Social Status: A desire for social status is a major factor in decision-making, particularly in the social media age. Whether called fear of missing out, keeping up with the Kardashians, succumbing to peer pressure or ego tripping, human beings strive for social status -- to be accepted and admired. While not inherently bad, such pressure can lead to sub-optimal financial decisions.

Procrastination: A high degree of procrastination results when people feel uncomfortable with a task, especially when faced with it for the first time. The complexity of the task gets blown out of proportion and people delay, delay, delay. Sometimes the task never gets started, even with the best of intentions. New financial tasks are especially scary.

Overconfidence: Most are over confident in their abilities. For example, one study of US drivers showed that 82% perceive themselves in the top 30% of all drivers in terms of safety -- a statistical impossibility. In the context of spending, many think they can control and maximize their resources without making any effort or paying attention. Maybe some rare, highly gifted individuals can. For the rest of us mere mortals, tracking dollars and using a consistent management process produces a better result. While confidence is a good thing and most over-confidence is harmless, when making financial decisions it is better to be skeptical and precise.

Immediate Gratification: Most would rather be entertained in the present and work in the future. Most prefer to save tomorrow and spend today.

Psychological Solutions

The good news is that we are not helpless in the face of our imperfect human wiring. To overcome these psychological roadblocks, establish clear priorities with frequent feedback and positive reinforcement.

Process Puts Money in Your Pocket: Improve spending efficiency by using a regular monitoring process. Do not assume. Gathering the information allows financial decisions to be put into context, dramatically improving the result even without perfectly rational decision-making. Let the process work and expect to see improvement each month.

Frequent Feedback Keeps You on Track: Frequently measuring actual results versus targets improves the outcome -- a shorter feedback loop delivers better results. Reviewing the data once per year is preferred to never analyzing spending patterns. Monthly measurement is better than an annual review. Weekly is better than monthly.

The more often the data are reviewed, the more easily the individual can adjust to events and recalibrate. For example, if a capital account deposit of $700 was a particular month's goal, but only $500 was actually deposited, then questions should be asked. What did not occur as expected? Should any changes be made to either behavior or to expectations? Do not expect perfection; adjust and move on.

Stay Focused on You: Do not worry about social status and do not obsess to distraction about what others are posting on social media. Compete with yourself -- aim for your goals, not the goals of others. While easier said than done, do not let friends hold you back. It is nice to be wildly popular, but it is better to be happy and financially self-sufficient.

Start -- Do Not Delay: Create specific action items to accomplish today, this week and this month. Understand that financial management is a process, not a one time exercise. Do not stress about the outcome or assume that everything has to be perfect. Start, let the process work and shoot for continuous improvement.

Expect to Succeed: Set achievable goals. Do not expect too much too soon. Short-term goals should be specific, written down and actionable. Make a weekly or monthly to do list and cross off items when completed. Establish long-term goals, but understand that these are more directional in nature and less actionable. Make certain that short-term goals are consistent with long-term objectives.

Reward Yourself: Unless you are a monk living in a monastery, enjoying life and having the ability to be spontaneous are important. When a short-term target is hit, reward yourself. Waste some money on something you enjoy. Have fun.

Stay the Course: Consistency over time is essential. Some months will exceed expectations, some will be disastrous and most will come in close to plan. Whatever the result, make adjustments and stay with the program. Creating a virtuous financial cycle, defined as positive monthly cash flow and continually increasing net worth, is the objective. Maintain forward motion.

Once a management process has been established, psychological roadblocks can be overcome. The good news is that most typically report better than expected results, creating a win-win -- more money for fun and more cash in the capital account.

STEP III: TAKE CONTROL

Take your expense worksheet and question each expense line item. Start with the largest dollar category, usually housing expenses, and sequentially work down to the smallest. Not surprisingly, toothpaste at approximately $3.00 per tube is far down the list.

Identify Alternatives

Americans generally overpay for goods and services. The good news hidden in this sad but true fact is a significant opportunity to reduce spending without affecting lifestyle. The mission is to question each spending decision, consciously looking for better ways to use hard-earned cash.

Make sure to distinguish between a need and a want when identifying alternatives. A need is a product that is a must, an absolute requirement. Unless living in a city with convenient subway or bus transportation, a car for transportation to and from work is an example of a necessity. The least expensive car in the market fulfills the transportation need. The want is an upgraded, more costly version of the need -- what we desire and aspire to purchase. The Mercedes Benz sedan, costing five or six times the least expensive car and even more to insure and operate, is the want satisfying the transportation requirement at a dramatically higher cost. Madison Avenue and peer pressure constantly push us to purchase the more expensive want. Try to separate the cost of the "want" from the cost of fulfilling the "need" for each item.

Ask the question, "Do less expensive alternatives of similar quality exist?" Be careful when answering, as many assume that the more expensive item is always the higher quality item; the less expensive item is perceived to be qualitatively cheaper only because it costs less.

Clear your mind of Don Draper's Madison Avenue conditioning and determine if other lower-cost, high quality branded products can be substituted. As discussed, toothpaste is a good example of a category with multiple branded products. On our commissary list, Close-Up sells for a lot less than Colgate and, as far as I can tell, the guys that buy Close-Up have the same number of teeth and minty fresh breath as Colgate customers.

Does a generic product exist at a lower price that delivers the same functional utility as the branded item? An example that I use to make the point is peanuts. Planters' Peanuts is a great product, but is it worth the extra money versus a generic brand such as Kirkland's sold at Costco? Although not a "peanut sommelier" by any means, after taking a blind taste test, I could not tell the difference between the two. In this instance, the savings may be peanuts, but remember that every little bit adds up.

Housing is not as easy an analysis as small dollar items like toothpaste or peanuts. The cost of the roof overhead is usually one's largest monthly check, typically involves a legal contract (lease or home purchase mortgage) dictating terms and limiting flexibility of substitution, and depends on local real estate market conditions. Furthermore, family status is a major factor in housing decisions and is a significant flexibility limiting factor. All that said, housing costs must be managed. After all, it is the biggest check most write each month.

Distinguish between the want and the need when making housing decisions. A roof overhead is a need. A 20,000 square foot home on the beach is a want. If you are in the wealth building stage, opt for the roof. If you have already amassed wealth like our UPS employee with $70 million, then go for the beach house. Be careful not to let peer pressure push you into an overly expensive housing situation. If already in a bad situation, then immediately explore ways to move. If renting, explore subletting. If a home owner with monthly costs that are too high, downsize as quickly as possible.

Make sure to examine the costs of debt relationships and explore alternatives. For example, many mortgages include a monthly fee for mortgage payment insurance which can often be eliminated as time passes and equity builds. Also, market conditions may permit a mortgage refinance that reduces interest charges and monthly payments. Credit card companies do not charge the same annual interest rates or card membership fees. Identify the least expensive credit card available.

List all viable substitute products on the expense worksheet and then calculate the monthly and annual savings for each. Add up the total potential savings when finished -- the total may surprise you.

HAVE IT YOUR WAY

For years, Burger King successfully used the advertising slogan - Have It Your Way - to tell customers that a Burger King burger could be customized to their specifications, as a clear point of differentiation from their main competition, McDonald's.

Have It Your Way encapsulates the right sentiment for this stage of the expense control process as each individual must have it their way or their efforts will produce disappointing results.

Have It Your Way acknowledges that no singular spending recipe is the "right way." Each person's situation -- income potential, expense structure, aspirations and desires -- is unique. One size does not fit all. Each person requires and deserves a custom-tailored program to maximize their happiness.

Establishing spending priorities is a personal choice. One person can decide to be brutally cost-efficient in one product category, providing low psychic benefit, and spend lavishly in another that matters emotionally. Another person can choose to do the exact opposite. As long as net spending achieves the individual's overall target, both are "right."

Prioritizing spending so that pleasurable activities can be funded along with necessities is the only way to stay with the program over the long haul. As my young bride constantly reminded me, one does not live by positive cash flow alone. Having it your way is the solution.

Most fiscally prudent people adhere to this concept, consciously or not. I have a friend who is profoundly sensible when it comes to money, spending well below his capability. Yet, even he has one expense category that he enjoys so much that he spends exponentially more than the average guy -- golf. He loves it. Nothing makes him happier than to be on the golf course walking the fairways on a bright, sunny afternoon with his two boys.

Does he spend more than he "should" on golf? Probably, but my thought is, "Right On."

Not every one loves golf, but everyone typically has at least one product or service that offers great satisfaction and personal enjoyment. Spoiling yourself is good and, importantly, it is not inconsistent with positive cash flow.

What cannot happen is to let everyone else have it THEIR WAY with your money, not the ad men, not your friends and not family members. You can overpay on some product categories, but not all. Balance is required. Trade-offs must be decided upon. Consciously ranking priorities is the key to achieving balance.

Take the expense worksheet with all the identified alternatives and prioritize. Decide which items you want to substitute a more dollar efficient product for, which ones you want to reduce the purchasing frequency of and which items you want to eliminate entirely. Is there a category that you want to spend more on? Keep playing with the alternatives until achieving your Double Time savings objective.

ACT -- NO TALKING AND NO THINKING -- ACT

The key is to act. You have done the fact gathering, contemplated normal human foibles and solutions, and calculated how to achieve your goal. You have a laser-like focus on the dollar destination. Identify easy areas -- toothpaste and peanuts for example -- and get moving. Take it item by item and build momentum and a sense of accomplishment. Grab the easy savings and move on to the tougher ones.

Part III
Do Not Save

1

No Parking

Watching cash build up due to mastering the concept of positive cash flow is a beautiful feeling: your financial muscle grows with each deposit.

The next step in the process is white knuckle time for most. Deciding what to do with an ever growing cash balance can be frightening and bewildering. The vast majority of Americans have never been taught the basics of investing in school or at home. When you add in a financial industry that does its best to make everything complicated and full of jargon, it is no wonder people feel immensely unsettled when considering what to do with their money.

The prevailing financial wisdom for most Americans can be summarized as: live within your means and put the excess cash in savings. While not wrong per se, I believe this two part "wisdom" to be flawed and incomplete.

First, as discussed in the prior section, the term living within your means is too limiting and tends to convince people to accept their current position in life and not dream for more. People should have dreams and challenge themselves to figure out a way to achieve them.

Second, while parking cash in a bank account is generally a necessary step, leaving cash in a checking or savings account or even in a slightly higher yielding bank certificate of deposit ("CD") for any length of time creates a guaranteed loss of purchasing power; a fact that most do not appreciate. That is why bank savings accounts should be renamed "guaranteed losing" accounts.

Everyone has two lucrative potential sources of income: the paycheck from a job and the money made from a capital account. Most Americans work very hard for their paycheck, but most neglect the second source. Most do not understand how important and easy it is to make their money work hard for them.

In recent years, there has been a lot of media attention about widening income inequality in the United States between the richest and poorest Americans. One of the major drivers of the increasing gap is the fact that the value of assets, such as homes and stocks, have grown faster than income from wages. As a result, individuals who do not own homes or invest in the stock market are getting left behind. Interestingly, this phenomenon is not unique to the United States or new. A 2017 study by 4 economists studied financial data from 16 countries finding similar trends, as does the popular 2013 book "Capital in the Twenty-First Century" by economist Thomas Piketty.

For working Americans, the call to action is urgent: create a second source of income through investing or risk getting left behind as income inequality grows.

The demise of the company sponsored pension plan and the rise of its replacements, the 401(k) account and self directed Individual Retirement Accounts, raises the stakes even higher. A person's retirement nest egg is dependent on the individual making intelligent investment choices.

The good news is that the US stock and bond markets are open to all at any time. Cash is all you need to get into the game and reap the benefits.

INFLATION -- STUFF COSTS MORE EACH YEAR

A key economic fact is that the prices of goods and services change every year. Some goods go up in price and some go down in price as economic conditions dictate. For example, when the price of oil drops in the world market, the price of gasoline at the pump in Ohio will typically decline shortly after. If wages paid to workers rise, then companies will typically raise the prices they charge in order to stay in business.

Governments track and compile the changes and aggregate them to come up with a factor for the average change in prices at the consumer level; in the United States it is called the Consumer Price Index ("CPI"). Typically this information is quoted as a year over year percentage change. Inflation occurs when the CPI has increased from the prior period and deflation occurs when the general price level has declined on a year-over-year basis. A 2% inflation rate means that the average price for goods and services increased by 2% versus the prior year.

Inflation, prices increasing year over year, has been an economic fact of life in the United States since 1933 when, in the midst of the Great Depression, the US stopped backing the value of each dollar with a set amount of gold. In fact, there has not been a single year since 1955 in which the Consumer Price Index has declined.[*] From 1990 to 2009, the average annual increase in the CPI has been 2.8%.[**]

---

[*] Siegel, Jeremy J., *Stocks for the Long Run.* 2014 Fifth edition, page 211.
[**] *Ilmanen, Antti. Expected Returns.* 2011, page 25, Table 2.1.

The table below shows how a 2.8% annual rate of increase in prices affects purchasing power.

Base Year Purchasing Power	Amount Required to Maintain Purchasing Power	
	Year 5	Year 10
$1,000	$1,148	$1,318

Your salary needs to increase by the rate of inflation, or purchasing power will shrink and you can buy less. After 10 years of inflation averaging 2.8% per year, the same $1,000 buys approximately 25% less. If your salary does not keep pace, you are poorer.

Similarly, to create wealth (i.e. more purchasing power) and get ahead in the capital account, the account value must grow by at least the annual rate of inflation.

DO NOT SAVE -- INVEST

Saving money on a monthly basis is the important first step to financial freedom. Parking those funds in a bank account for a few days is completely acceptable. However, leaving money in a savings or checking account for any length of time is a waste.

To understand this point, think of a parking meter on the street. Parking a car at the meter and dropping a coin in the slot is the intelligent thing to do. Access to the vehicle is convenient and the cost is minimal. However, if you leave a car at a meter after it has expired, then a meter maid will stick a $30 or $50 parking ticket under the windshield wiper. Leave it for too long and the car gets towed, incurring even more fees. All of a sudden, a good deal became a really bad deal because you stayed too long.

Parking long-term capital is exactly the same. Parking in a bank is fine for a short period, but the money must be moved to a better, more productive location before too long.

Why? Traditionally, banks have paid lower annual rates of interest on savings accounts than the annual rate of price inflation. Today, the relationship is approximately 0.4% for savings type accounts and approximately 2.2% for the annual rise in prices. Assuming these rates, money left for 5 years in a savings account loses approximately 9% of its purchasing power -- meaning nearly 10% less stuff can be bought with the same dollars. Leave the money in for 10 years and the decline in purchasing power equals approximately 16%. If retirement money is left in the bank for 40 years, then the saver loses approximately half his purchasing power.

This is just the opposite of making your cash work hard for you. Think of it as letting your money lay on the beach sipping margaritas while you work harder and harder to pay the bills.

Most do not appreciate this phenomenon and when it is explained the response is usually, "Why didn't someone tell me this sooner?"

A real world example occurred shortly after my daughter graduated from high school when I suggested that she move the gift money that she had saved from holidays, birthdays and graduations out of her savings account and into a capital account. Her immediate reaction was, "What if I lose money?" It was an excellent question. I responded by asking her what her savings account was paying in terms of annual interest -- at that time 0.09% per year. I then asked if she knew what price inflation was -- "No." I went on to explain how she was already losing money due to inflation and was guaranteed to keep losing purchasing power unless a change was made. She opened the account the next day.

Significantly better options exist that allow capital to be more productive. In other words, stop paying for the margarita-soaked beach vacation and put that lazy capital to work.

As illustration, investing in AAA-rated US corporate loans (contractual obligations of America's financially strongest and most stable companies) historically has generated an average annual return several percentage points higher than inflation. Assuming a 4.0% total return on these bonds versus a 2.0% yearly inflation rate, purchasing AAA-rated corporate loans increases purchasing power and wealth. After 10 years purchasing power will increase by approximately 20% and after 40 years it will double.

Admittedly, moving out of the convenient, understandable and Federally guaranteed savings account involves risk of loss and uncertainty which makes many nervous. However, the comparison is straightforward. A savings account offers a certain, guaranteed loss of purchasing power. Investing in stocks and bonds has historically generated profits significantly in excess of inflation, but comes with uncertainty. Prices fluctuate and profits are not guaranteed.

The only way to create wealth is to understand the risks and rewards of different types of investments, take a deep, calming breath and get started. Do not save -- invest.

2

Investing

Hopefully, you are convinced that parking long-term money in a low yielding savings account is a losing proposition and that investing in higher profit producing investments is the only way to build wealth. The question then becomes what to invest in: What are the choices, how much profit can one expect from each and how much risk is involved?

Pick up *The Wall Street Journal, Barron's* or even the business section of the *USA Today* and you will see pages of numbers -- prices and percentages spanning multiple investment categories and thousands of individual stocks, bonds and commodities. The choices are so numerous and bewildering that the beginner is often intimidated.

This section explains in plain language the major categories of investments that the average investor should consider and describes fundamental concepts by which to evaluate each.

MAJOR ASSET GROUPS

The pages and pages of numbers in the financial press can be simplified into three major categories of investments: ownership interests in companies ("stocks"), ownership interests in real estate and commodities ("real assets") and loans ("fixed income investments") where the investor purchases part of a loan (becoming a lender) to a government, state, municipality or company.

PUBLIC VERSUS PRIVATE

In each category, the investor can purchase interests in publicly traded securities or in the securities of private entities.

<u>Public</u>

The focus of this book is investing in publicly traded, passive stock and fixed income investments. Real assets are contemplated only in terms of buying stocks and loans of publicly traded real estate entities. We do not discuss investing in currencies, commodities, metals, options, futures, annuities or other derivatives of these basic categories. These types of investments are complicated and can be highly volatile and are best left to professionals.

The individual can invest in publicly traded stocks and fixed income securities and can purchase real estate interests and other real assets on national exchanges. Investing in publicly traded securities is often referred to as "passive investing" because the investor does not take on the day-to-day management of the company or the piece of real estate. The investor risks hard earned money, but does not take on any additional responsibilities.

Virtually all the prices listed in the financial press are for publicly traded securities and are considered passive investments.

Importantly, these investments are liquid meaning they can be bought and sold cheaply and quickly. All the investor has to do is log on to a brokerage account and type in a few key strokes to buy and sell.

The most attractive feature of investing in the public capital markets for those just starting to invest is the ability to get on the wealth creation train for as little as $100.

<u>Private</u>

The alternative, investing in the stocks or loans of privately held companies, is very difficult for the individual and nearly impossible for someone just starting out. Investing in private entities typically requires significant amounts of money, considerable and relevant industry expertise and some amount of financial savvy. These investments are illiquid, meaning active markets with quoted prices do not exist. They are time consuming and difficult to identify and expensive to purchase and sell.

Individuals can and frequently do invest in real assets in private transactions, particularly real estate. Here too, the investor must take on significantly more responsibility for the asset. In the case of real estate, he must locate the property, negotiate the purchase price and contract of sale, source a mortgage loan, typically provide a personal guarantee of the mortgage, lease the property to tenants, handle tenant issues, prepare financial statements and tax filings, and more. The individual is responsible for all aspects of management of the asset.

Investing in private assets can be quite lucrative -- and should be -- if successful: the investor is actively managing the asset and must be compensated for the additional headaches and risks. The extra profit from these types of investments is often referred to as "sweat equity."

Part III - A
Stocks

1

Owning a Company

Growing up in Ohio in the late 1960's, our neighbor, Mr. Jansen, would occasionally take my brother and me to McDonald's. It was always a treat because McDonald's at that time was a very recent phenomenon. Every time we walked in our local "Golden Arches" with him, he would say, "I own these glass doors." At first, I did not pay attention or care what he meant. After several more visits with him saying the same thing, I asked my dad what it meant. My dad explained that Mr. Jansen owned shares of stock in the company that operated our McDonald's. Dad went on to explain that Mr. Jansen owned a very small part of the company. His way of expressing that concept, as well as his pride of ownership, was to say that he owned the glass doors. The truth is that I did not understand what either of them told me until many years later when I started to learn about stock ownership.

Mr. Jansen was right. Buying a share of stock of a publicly traded company makes you an owner of that company. The purchaser is legally entitled to all the benefits of ownership that accrue to each share of stock for as long as it is owned. The most important economic benefit is the shareholder's claim on the assets of the company and a share in its profits.

Many of America's greatest companies are listed on United States' stock exchanges with ownership shares trading daily, including Apple, Microsoft, Walmart, McDonald's, Bank of America, Facebook, Home Depot, Amazon, Ford Motor, Johnson & Johnson, and Exxon. In total, nearly 4,000 companies are listed on exchanges in the United States. More than 30 countries around the world maintain stock exchanges and post prices for ownership interests in their listed companies. Altogether, there are approximately 19,000 companies worldwide whose shares can be bought and sold on an exchange.

An individual who desires to be an owner of McDonald's or Amazon or another public company can place an order electronically, complete the trade within minutes and begin to reap the benefits of ownership.

THE STOCK PRICE

The prices listed in the paper or quoted online are for one share of stock. For example, if Bank of America is trading at $28.50, then one share of Bank of America can be bought for that price plus brokerage fees. To buy 100 shares, the investor would have to spend $2,850 ($28.50 x 100) plus any trading costs and commissions. To buy 1,000 shares, the total cost would be $28,500 plus fees.

To purchase 100% of Bank of America's stock and own the company completely, one has to buy all the shares issued and outstanding. In the case of Bank of America with approximately 10 billion shares outstanding, owning 100% would cost $285 billion ($28.50 x 10 billion shares). This $285 billion total is called Bank of America's "market value" or its "market capitalization." Market value is the total value that the stock market puts on a company.

An investor who owns 1,000 shares of Bank of America stock owns a tiny fraction of the entire company and has many fellow shareholders. To put this in Mr. Jansen's terms, if he owned 1,000 shares of Bank of America today, Mr. Jansen would probably say that he owned the handle on a bank branch's front door.

No matter how big or small the ownership percentage, each shareholder receives the same economic rights and benefits, including per share profits and any cash paid out of profits to shareholders.

People buy stocks with the expectation that the price of the shares will go up as the company grows.

BUYING STOCKS

Shares of public companies are listed on an exchange, where buyers and sellers converge to trade. The purpose of the exchange is to facilitate the efficient transfer of securities between buyer and seller. Historically, trading took place on exchange floors, but trading is almost entirely electronic now.

In the United States, the majority of stocks are listed either on the New York Stock Exchange or what is called NASDAQ, the National Association of Securities Dealers' Automated Quotation system. When the financial news networks televise the ringing of the bell ceremony which starts and ends the stock trading day, the people pushing the bell are at one of these two exchanges in New York City.

An individual cannot trade directly on the exchange. Your broker maintains a relationship with the exchange and communicates orders on a client's behalf to the market makers of the stock of interest. The market maker provides a continuous price at which it will buy (bid) and a price at which it will sell (ask) the stock. The difference between the bid and the ask prices is called the bid/ask spread. The bid/ask spread represents the market maker's fee on trades. Typically, a stock with more shares trading on a daily basis has a smaller bid/ask spread, meaning that the cost to trade in that stock is less per share than that of companies that trade less frequently.

To make a trade with a full service broker, the client places a phone call to his broker and explains his wishes. The broker then enters the order into the firm's system and when the trade is complete calls the client with the particulars -- shares purchased or sold, share price, commission incurred and the total cash involved in the transaction.

To trade with an online broker like Fidelity or Charles Schwab, the client logs onto his account and enters the required information to complete the transaction. Having helped many make their first trade, I know that most are slightly anxious and worried about making a mistake. Do not be. It is an easy process, with understandable prompts and questions, that takes a minute or two to complete. If a problem does arise, the online brokers have telephone support personnel available 24 hours a day. Each online broker's transaction screens are slightly different, so the description here is by necessity a generic one.

The first step is to click on the header titled something like, "Make a Trade." A screen will pop up that will prompt the client for the required information. The first piece of information needed is the "ticker symbol" for the stock, often shortened to just the "ticker" or the "symbol." The ticker symbol is a stock's unique alphabetic name by which it is known in the market. Examples are listed below. If you do not know a particular company's ticker, a look up function is provided in which you enter the name of the company and the relevant ticker is displayed. Enter the ticker in the provided space.

Amazon: AMZN	General Electric: GE
Apple: AAPL	General Motors: GM
Bank of America: BAC	Home Depot: HD
Facebook: FB	McDonalds: MCD
Ford Motor: F	Xerox: XRX

Typically, a small window will appear that provides the current market activity for the stock symbol entered, including last sale price, the current bid/ask spread, the day's high and low sale prices and share volume. The next question is generally "Buy or Sell?" After that, the "amount" is required. The amount refers to the number of shares, not the dollar amount.

For example, to buy BAC (Bank of America) one would enter 50 or 100 in the amount line, representing 50 or 100 shares of BAC. At that point, the system will generate the dollar particulars of the proposed transaction. Again using BAC, for a 50 share purchase with an assumed price of $24 per share, the transaction will be displayed as $1,200 plus the firm's commission. Assuming a $4.95 commission, our hypothetical proposed BAC purchase totals $1,204.95. The commission represents 0.4% of the dollar amount of stock purchased.

The final question is the type of order desired. The investor chooses from a list of potential order types, which will include the two most frequently used -- a market order and a limit order.

A market order tells the broker to buy or sell at the best price currently in the market. A limit order puts a price restriction on the broker in completing the transaction. For example, buy 50 shares of BAC only if the price drops to $23.75 or below. Or, sell 50 BAC only at $24.50 or above. For most individuals entering small dollar transactions in actively traded names, the market order option is appropriate.

If the particulars of the trade are acceptable to the investor and the type of order is entered, the investor hits send or some comparable "get it done" command icon. When the transaction is complete, the investor will be notified electronically with the final details of the trade. For large, actively traded stocks, the transaction time can be seconds. For a market order for a listed stock of almost any size, the transaction generally takes no more than a few minutes to complete.

THE PROFIT EQUATION

If the share price increases, then the investor profits when the stock is sold, as illustrated.

Bank of America Stock		
	Purchase Date	12 Months Later
Price	$28.50	$32.50
Total Invested (100 Shares)	$2,850.00	$3,250.00

Change In Price: +$4.00 per share	
Profit	
Dollars (100 Shares)	$400
Percent Profit	14.0%

Shareholders also receive dividends paid by the company on shares owned. A dividend is a payment made to shareholders out of company profits. Dividends are not required to be paid and many public companies do not pay them. If they are paid, then they are generally paid quarterly (every 3 months) to shareholders.

Assuming Bank of America is paying a quarterly dividend of $0.12 per share, then the investor's total profit for the year holding period increases, as shown below.

Dividend	$0.12 x 4 = $0.48 per share per year
Amount Received	$0.48 x 100 shares = $48.00
Dividend Yield	$48.00/$2,850.00 = 1.7%

Total Profit	
Dollars	$400.00 + $48.00 = $448.00
Percent	$448.00/$2,850 = 15.7%

The investor's profit derives from two sources: the price change of the stock upon sale and the cash dividends paid to shareholders over the course of the applicable holding period.

INVESTOR'S PROFIT
=
Stock Price Increase
+
Dividend Payments

In the Bank of America example, the investor bought 100 shares at $28.50 per share, 12 months later sold 100 shares for a total of $3,250 and received cash dividends of $48.00 on 100 shares held for the 12 months. In total, a profit of $448.00 was earned for holding the stock for one year, representing a 15.7% gain on the investment.

If the Bank of America stock price had declined to $24.50 and the investor chose to sell the 100 shares, then a loss would have been realized.

Cost	$2,850
Sale Proceeds	$2,450
Profit (Loss) on Sale	($400)
Dividend Income	$48
Total Gain (Loss)	
Dollars	($352)
Percent	(12.4)%

Dividends represent current income for the shareholder holding the stock. In the Bank of America example, the investor is getting paid 1.7% per year (assuming no increase or decrease in the dividend) while the bank works to grow its business and profits. Generally, the higher the dividend yield, the more investors are enticed to own a stock.

Additionally, dividends cushion the investor's loss when a stock depreciates in value. In our example, investing in Bank of America's stock is a losing proposition if the sale price of the stock declines by more than the 1.7% received per year in dividends. If the stock price realized upon sale does not change at all over the holding period, then the investor gets a 1.7% per year profit (assuming the dividend remains constant).

Companies that pay dividends reduce the risk of owning the stock because less of the expected profit comes from less predictable future price appreciation.

SHARE PRICES MOVE UP AND DOWN

Share prices move up and down during the course of trading as shares change hands between buyers and sellers. For the largest, most actively traded companies, share prices change second to second. Over a 52-week period, the forces of supply and demand can create large swings in a company's share price.

For example, during one trading day in July 2018, Bank of America's stock traded approximately 66 million shares, 169,000 shares per minute. While a large number of shares, the day's trading represented a very small portion of Bank of America's market value, just 0.7% of the total market capitalization (approximately $1.9 billion of trades out of a total value of $285 billion). During that trading day, Bank of America's price ranged from a low of

$28.25 to a high of $28.83, with a last sale price of $28.65. Over the course of the prior 12 months, Bank of America's stock price traded between $22.75 and $33.05 per share.

As the data for Bank of America highlight, stock prices can move dramatically. On a typical day, the price of a stock can fluctuate by several percentage points. Over the course of a year, shares can fluctuate even more. Bank of America's shares traded 18% lower and 18% higher than the year's $27.90 midpoint. This mercurial price movement occurred even as the stock market as a whole was stable, as it was from July 2017 to July 2018, and Bank of America's business was increasing in profitability.

How is the investor to interpret these price movements? What drives stock prices?

Over the long run, stock price changes correspond to changes in corporate financial performance. Benjamin Graham, one of the most famous investors of all time, called the stock market a weighing machine in the long run. What it weighs are corporate profits. If a company's sales, profits and dividends increase significantly, then typically its stock price will increase significantly.

As a whole, the market has followed the trend line of aggregate corporate profits, with profits valued sensibly the majority of the time. However, there have been periods of extreme pessimism and extreme optimism when the market is valued at ridiculous levels, which, of course, are only obvious when looking in the rear view mirror. At those times, "experts" are always offering intelligent sounding reasons why "this time is different." Be careful when stock market valuations are at the extremes. If you hear the phrase "this time is different" to explain the extremes, be skeptical and deliberate.

In the short run, stock price moves can seem random, even nonsensical to the average person. Do a company's profits and economic prospects change second to second? In our example, did Bank of America's outlook change every minute of the trading day? Of course not. Then what moves stock prices every day?

The answer is supply and demand. Some explain stock market behavior in the short run by comparing it to a popularity contest. Like a popularity contest, many different motivations and emotions come into play, some rational and some irrational. As in a popularity contest, everyone gets a vote, logical or not. The votes, in the context of the stock market, are buy and sell orders which create the demand and supply that move the price of a stock. More buy orders and the price goes up. More sell orders and the price trades down.

Generally, orders are placed by investors based on their opinion of the economic future. What is a certain company's prospects for the next several years? How will the US economy fair over the coming year? Everyone has an opinion. It is these constantly changing opinions of the future by millions of investors around the world that make markets and result in stock prices fluctuating in a random manner.

The problem for the investor is that there is no accurate way to predict how all the opinions will play out in prices on a day-to-day basis. Millions of hours of computer time have been expended crunching trillions of pieces of historical market data searching for patterns as a way to predict future prices, all to no avail. No one can accurately and consistently predict the future in terms of either company performance or stock market price movement.

The intelligent course of action for the individual investor is to ignore the short-term and focus on the long-term. Make investments that take advantage of the stock market's historical propensity to reward stocks with certain characteristics and penalize others lacking those characteristics. Make stock investments that put the odds of success in your favor.

VOLATILITY: PRICE FLUCTUATIONS

The up and down movement in stock prices discussed above is referred to as volatility. Understanding a little about volatility is essential for the investor, especially the beginner, as a grasp of "normal" price moves will help eliminate rash, ill advised trades.

By way of analogy, new army recruits are put through rigorous and intense training for months to prepare them for what to expect when real bullets start flying. The intent of the training is not to make soldiers impervious to the natural fear of being injured, but rather to prepare them to be able to carry out their orders and not panic despite the fear they feel.

What scares investors is when prices fall dramatically or steadily -- referred to as downside volatility.

The *Oxford English Dictionary* defines volatile as "liable to change rapidly and unpredictably, ESPECIALLY FOR THE WORSE." While a general definition, this could have been written with stock market investors in mind. Unexpected upside surprises are generally welcomed by stock investors. Downside volatility is the frightening part because most people intensely dislike losing money.

The challenge is to control the natural fear of losing money and to continue to make solid decisions in the midst of market turmoil and falling values.

Understanding a few important facts relating to stock market fluctuations will help calm nerves.

First, individual stocks are more volatile than the market as a whole. Consequently, the number of individual stocks in a portfolio affects overall price swings. For example, holding one stock typically is a wild ride. Incrementally increasing the number of stocks owned incrementally decreases volatility. Once a portfolio holds about 30 stocks, it will have achieved enough diversification so that the portfolio's value experiences fluctuations similar to the market.

Second, the US stock market as a whole increased in value in approximately 67% of the years since 1890. Of course, this means that it decreased in value -- investors experienced declining prices -- 33% of the time. Including all the ups and downs, the US market historically generated a long-term average annual profit of around 10%. If losing money in one year causes sleepless nights and a 10% compound return is insufficient upside to compensate, then avoid stocks.

Third, the "normal" yearly fluctuation around the 10% average gain is +/- 18%. In statistical terms, this is called the standard deviation of the historical results. Standard deviation is a mathematical tool used to quantify the probability of the range of future returns compared to the historical average profit. Translated, it means that about 2/3 of the time the total return of the market in one year ranges from a profit of 28% to a loss of 8%.

About 90% of the time, the market return comes in between a gain of 46% and a loss of 26%. The remaining 10% of the periods produces returns on both ends of these numbers, some very high profits and some extreme losses. On the downside, the US market has declined more than 40% in a year 9 times since 1890, the last occurring in 2008.

Importantly, a longer holding period both increases the odds of making money and decreases the standard deviation of return, as shown in the chart below.

The likelihood of making money in stocks over extended periods of time is quite high -- the odds are in the investor's favor. Internalizing this fact is critical so that when the bullets start flying and the market drops suddenly, the long term investor remains composed and thinking clearly.

Annual Return Range				
Holding Period (Years)	Standard Deviation	Downside	Average	Upside
1	18%	-8%	+10%	+28%
2	12%	-2%	+10%	+22%
5	7%	+3%	+10%	+17%
10	4%	+6%	+10%	+14%
20	3%	+7%	+10%	+13%
30	2%	+8%	+10%	+12%

COMPANY VALUATION

The prices for stocks printed in *The Wall Street* Journal and quoted online represent the cost to purchase one share of stock. Scanning the daily list in the Wall Street Journal of the 1,000 largest US stocks shows prices for shares ranging all over the map. For example, in July 2017, Warren Buffet's public company, Berkshire Hathaway (Class A), was trading around $256,000 per share; to buy one share, the investor would need to spend $256,000 plus commissions.

Conversely, Under Armour, the athletic apparel company, was trading around $20.50 per share, requiring only $20.50 plus fees to buy one share. The $256,000 that buys one share of Berkshire Hathaway purchases approximately 12,488 shares of Under Armour. Clearly, Under Armour's price per share is significantly cheaper than Berkshire Hathaway's. But which is the better bargain for the investor?

When asked this question in class, nearly all students answer, "Under Armour because you get so many more shares for the same money." While accurate in terms of the number of shares, this answer could not be more wrong.

When I explain that Berkshire Hathaway is in fact the better deal, none of my students believe me, often expressing their disbelief loudly and in colorful language. The reaction is understandable as they are a cynical group, used to dealing with men in prison who frequently try to sell alternative facts and conspiracy theories. The Berkshire Hathaway/Under Armour example is a paradox: a statement that seems to conflict with common sense, but that is nevertheless true. After they quiet down, I explain how stocks are valued by investors.

To value a stock, the price paid must be compared to some measure of that company's economic production. As an owner of the company, the shareholder receives a pro rata percentage of any distributed cash based on his ownership percentage, not on what was paid for the ownership percentage. Hence, it is in the buyer's best interest to pay as little as possible per dollar of economic production for the stock. A comparison of price to financial fundamentals permits stocks of different share prices and companies of varying sizes to be compared on an apples-to-apples basis.

The most commonly used company valuation measure is the price-to-earnings ratio or the P/E ratio. The P/E ratio compares a stock's share price to its yearly profit per share, commonly called its earnings per share or EPS, which all public companies are required to publish quarterly.

PRICE / EARNINGS RATIO

Price of One Share

Divided By

Earnings (Profits) of the Company for One Share

The fundamental basis of a stock's value derives from the amount of cash expected to be received in future years by the shareholder, discounted back to the present. Since cash typically can not be distributed to shareholders unless the company makes a profit, a company's earnings and the expected growth in earnings drive valuations.

Let's use the P/E ratio to compare the market's valuation of Berkshire Hathaway and Under Armour in July 2017 and answer the question as to which is the better buy. Berkshire Hathaway's share price was $256,000 and its yearly profits were approximately $13,474 per share, resulting in a P/E ratio of 19x. Under Armour's stock was trading at $20.50 and its yearly profits were about $0.40 per share, resulting in a P/E ratio of 51x.

A great way to think of the P/E ratio concept is in terms of payback times. Assuming each company pays out 100% of yearly profits to shareholders, it takes a Berkshire Hathaway shareholder 19 years to get paid back and 51 years for an Under Armour investor to get repaid. I ask the class, "Which would you prefer, getting all your money back in 19 years or 51 years?" Again, all the students give the same answer -- 19 years, but this time they are right.

Even if Under Armour grows its profits at 20% per year versus 10% per year for Berkshire Hathaway, the Berkshire Hathaway shareholder's payback time is shorter. At these growth rates, it takes a little over 12 years for the Under Armour investor to get repaid compared to a little over 10 years for the Berkshire Hathaway shareholder.

Berkshire Hathaway is significantly cheaper than Under Armour on a cost per dollar of profit basis: with a P/E ratio of 19x versus 51x, and most likely a faster payback even factoring earnings growth into the picture. Berkshire Hathaway is the better value.*

---

* Six months later in January 2018, Berkshire Hathaway stock had increased 25% and Under Armour's stock had decreased 30%.

VALUATION RATIOS

Investors use a variety of different financial ratios to determine the value of a stock as compared to other stocks. Typically, if a company's stock is inexpensive using one ratio, then it will also be inexpensive using other valuation ratios. In some cases, however, a company's performance needs to be reviewed from a variety of perspectives to get at the true value.

A listing and brief explanation of the principal ratios used by professional investors to value companies can be found in Appendix C.

One of my favorite investment books, *What Works on Wall Street* by James P. O'Shaughnessy, analyzes how a range of financial valuation ratios reflect subsequent investment performance. The research shows that in the case of each of these ratios, the stocks exhibiting better valuation relationships today delivered higher profits to the investor in the future.

The investor would be wise to avoid expensively valued stocks, the glamour stocks, in favor of cheaper, value stocks. Once in a blue moon an exceedingly expensive stock, like Amazon, will do well in the marketplace over an extended time period. Understand that Amazon is the rare exception; for every Amazon there are 10 or 20 others that do not deliver enough in the future to justify lofty valuations today.

TECHNICAL ANALYSIS

Technical Analysis, another analytical approach to the stock market, studies historical price action and trading volumes of a stock or the broader market in an attempt to predict the future. Books have been written arguing both in support of and against this form of analysis. Thousands of seminars have been offered extolling and teaching the techniques -- for a fee, of course. Billions of hours of computer time have been dedicated to picking apart past price data for clues on the movement of future prices. Despite all this effort, there has not been a speck of evidence that anyone or any computer can predict stock prices accurately and consistently.

Often, individuals who trade in and out of stocks on a daily basis ("day traders") convince themselves that they can read the market and know where it is going. Notwithstanding all the jargon they spout, the reality is that day traders are making a guess as to price direction and reacting quickly to sell and limit losses if the guess is wrong. This is not investing; it is more akin to playing a roulette wheel in a casino. In both cases, the odds of success are not in your favor. If someone pitches you on day trading, nod politely and walk quickly in the other direction.

Day trading and the false promise of fast riches is a problem I have to overcome in every investing class I teach. For some reason, the typical Federal inmate equates the stock market with in and out trading and wants to learn the magic formula. I usually lose a few students after I explain that my class is not about day trading and, furthermore, that I have seen no evidence or research studies that show that consistently successful day trading is possible.

Interestingly, there is evidence that one style of investing that relies purely on price action does work and, moreover, has been the subject of academic research and computer back testing. It is called momentum investing.

Momentum investing involves buying stocks that have risen in price and selling those that have fallen. The strategy is not premised on predicting future prices, certainly not the next day's price. Nor is it a growth stock strategy, which involves buying high-flying, fast-growing story stocks. Rather, it seeks to benefit from the tendency of stocks to continue their directional momentum higher or lower -- in the short run. Unlike guessing future price moves, momentum investing involves a set of precise, quantifiable rules as to when to buy and sell.

The strategy can be summarized as: recent winners (stocks with rising prices) continue to win; recent losers (stocks with falling prices) continue to fall. It is important to note that both directional trends occur for relatively short periods of time and then disappear.

The momentum investing concept is straightforward, has produced profits for investors and can be replicated. The problem with this type of investing is that it is calculation intensive, as each stock and its price must be tracked constantly, and expensive to execute as portfolios must be rebalanced frequently incurring significant trading costs. Furthermore, the majority of the gains are short-term in nature, resulting in higher tax obligations.

Until recently, momentum investing strategies were strictly for the professional investor as the sophistication required and the associated costs were prohibitive for the individual investor. Recently, exchange traded funds employing momentum disciplines were made available to the investing public by reputable sponsors. As a result, the individual investor can now access this strategy efficiently.

STOCK DIVERSIFICATION

In the context of stock investing, putting all your eggs in one basket (buying one stock) is not recommended. Spreading stock investment dollars across a number of stocks reduces the risk of ownership and is called diversification. Most professional financial advisors recommend holding a minimum of 30-35 individual companies for proper diversification of a stock portfolio. Note, however, that even a properly diversified portfolio does not eliminate risk, only reduces it. The investor is still exposed to market risk-- the volatility of the overall stock market.

Attaining adequate diversification was historically a challenge for the individual investor just starting out or with a small account balance. Buying even one share of 30 or 35 stocks required too much cash and associated brokerage commissions and bid/ask spread costs were so onerous that the prospect of a decent return was eliminated.

Fortunately, this has changed dramatically in the last 50 years in favor of the little guy. Financial firms introduced investment products that the individual could access with as little as $100 and still be diversified. These products are called mutual funds and exchange traded funds ("ETFs"). In addition, brokerage commissions are significantly lower and bid/ask spreads have narrowed, making trading more dollar efficient. This change is often referred to as the "democratization" of the financial markets. There has never been a better time for the little guy to invest.

The introduction of mutual funds and more recently the introduction of ETFs solved the diversification issue for the small investor, making stock market investing dramatically easier and more efficient. Mutual funds and ETFs are professionally managed and invest according to a stated and legally binding investment objective. The funds sell shares to investors, aggregate the money into one big pot or pool, and purchase stocks according to the fund's investment objective. Investors share in the investment profits or losses of the fund on a pro rata basis according to ownership.

In class, we call these products "bundles" or, when referring to stock funds, "stock bundles."

2

Stock Bundles

For the first 3 or 4 years teaching stock market concepts, I referred to mutual and exchange traded funds as "professionally managed pools of capital." While an accurate description, my students did not quickly grasp the concept of investment funds until we started to call them "bundles."

The word was coined one day while we were discussing funds when a student shouted from the back of the room, "Oh, you mean like a bundle, a bundle of stocks." The other guys immediately jumped on the word and our class descriptor of "bundles" was born.

The dictionary definition of a bundle is a package of things wrapped together for convenience, often offered for sale at a package price.

This is exactly what a stock mutual fund or an exchange traded fund is. While each has a unique investment objective, all funds package stocks together for the convenience of the investor and offer these packages for sale.

Available stock bundles currently number in the thousands and, like stocks, each carries an alphabetic ticker symbol as an identifier. Also like individual stocks, share prices for bundles differ, but are generally affordable for the individual investor.

Share prices as high as Berkshire Hathaway's $256,000 do not exist and would defeat the purpose of making bundles easily accessible for individuals. For example, on July 28, 2017 of the 100 largest exchange traded funds listed in *The Wall Street Journal*, the highest closing share price was $322.41 for the SPDR S&P MidCap Index fund (ticker: MDY). Most trade between $25 and $100 per share.

Some bundles mirror the major market indexes like the SPDR Dow Jones Industrial Average Trust (ticker: DIA) consisting of 30 very large US companies or the SPDR S&P 500 Index exchange traded fund (ticker: SPY) composed of 500 large US companies. These funds own the exact configuration of the companies in the Average or Index to replicate its investment performance for the investor.

Some bundles are run by money managers who actively pick the specific stocks included in the portfolio based on their own particular investment philosophy, with a goal of beating or at least matching a benchmark's profit performance. Examples include the Fidelity Contrafund (ticker: FCNTX) run by Will Danoff, a famous and highly successful manager, and Fidelity's Low Price Stock Fund (ticker: FLPSX) run by another famous stock picker, Joel Tillinghast. The Dodge & Cox Stock Fund (ticker: DODGX), a very successful fund, is an example of another management structure in which stocks in the portfolio are selected by a team of investors rather than a single "star" manager.

Some target a specific industry group, such as biotechnology, utilities or energy, and others select stocks based on the major investment styles of value, growth or momentum.

Some stock bundles include only 20 companies in the package, like the Deep Value ETF (ticker: DVP), and some include hundreds of companies.

Some focus exclusively on US listed companies while others focus on stocks of companies headquartered in other countries or regions.

Other bundles sort companies and invest based on size of market capitalization, referred to as large cap, mid-cap or small cap funds.

Some stock bundles combine investment strategies and styles such as a US, mid-cap, value bundle or a European company value fund.

MARKET BUNDLES

Every day *CNN, Fox News, USA Today* and every other major news outlet post prices for the US stock market, listing the Dow Jones Industrial Average, the S&P 500 Index and the NASDAQ Composite Index. Most viewers and readers have no idea what these numbers represent, reacting solely to the green (up) or the red (down) arrows or the newscaster's tone of voice when describing the day's trading. An explanation of the market averages is one of the first topics we cover in class.

Each of the big three, the Dow, the S&P 500 and the NASDAQ, are slightly different in composition, but all are used to measure and calibrate stock market performance. Think of them as a needle on a car's speedometer informing the driver how fast the car is traveling. Just as the speedometer does not provide a driver all the information necessary to drive safely, the market averages, while useful, do not give the investor all the data required to invest safely.

Our class terminology for these indicators is Market Bundle. A Market Bundle is a group of individual stocks combined to form an average or index that is consistently quantified and monitored. A Market Bundle gives the investor information as to the market's direction and value. Note that these averages do not include all publicly traded stocks, just a subset. For example, the 500 stocks in the S&P 500 represent about 13% of the approximately 3,800 listed US companies. It is also important to understand that the components of bundles change over time. As the US economy changes and industries evolve, companies are added and deleted.

The Dow, the oldest of the market bundles, dates back to an 1896 introduction. Presumably it was formed for analytical and marketing purposes. Analysts want to gauge the price level and momentum of the market relative to corporate earnings and economic activity. The marketer and the press want an easy to quote, single numeric to communicate the health of the market to consumers of the news. The Dow is a point of reference for both.

When the question is asked, "What did the stock market do today?" The answer is usually given in terms of the Dow's performance despite the fact that it currently represents only about 25% of the US market's total dollar value and less than 1% of listed companies.

Since 1928, the Dow has consisted of 30 very large US companies. While the total has been constant since then, the make-up of the 30 has evolved. The most recent change occurred in 2018 when Walgreen's Boots Alliance was added and General Electric was dropped. In July 2018, the Dow was trading around 25,000; a 1% move in the average is represented by a 250 point change.

The current Dow components are listed below.

3M	Exxon Mobil	Nike
American Express	Goldman Sachs	Pfizer
Apple	Home Depot	Proctor & Gamble
Boeing	IBM	Travelers
Caterpillar	Intel	United Technologies
Chevron	Johnson & Johnson	United Health
Cisco Systems	McDonald's	Verizon
Coca Cola	Merck	Visa
Disney	Microsoft	Walgreen's Boots
DuPont	Morgan, J.P.	Wal-Mart Stores

The S&P 500, introduced in 1957, is a bundle of 500 large US companies in 11 industry groups. The 500 companies included in the Index are not a static group. Each year companies are added and subtracted. Since its inception in 1957, approximately 1,200 companies have been added and deleted from the S&P 500. The S&P 500 is a market capitalization weighted index, currently representing just under 75% of the total dollar value of the US market.

Because of its breadth, the S&P 500 is the preferred yardstick to measure the performance of the broad US stock market. As such, it is the benchmark against which the performance of mutual and exchange traded funds typically are compared. In July 2018, the S&P 500 was trading around 2800; a 28 point move translates into approximately a 1% change.

The NASDAQ, which stands for the National Association of Securities Dealers Automated Quotation system, was established in February 1971 when the computer terminals of market makers across the country were linked electronically for the first time. Today, virtually all stock trading is electronic. In July 2018, the NASDAQ was trading around 7800; a 1% move equaled approximately 78 points.

The NASDAQ Composite Index is market capitalization weighted, tracking the performance of all stocks traded on NASDAQ. Traditionally, NASDAQ has been home to younger, less established companies with a significant proportion of technology, medical products, biotechnology and regional banking companies. Prominent listings include Amazon, Apple, Biogen, Facebook, Google, Netflix and Tesla. Companies listed on NASDAQ and included in the Composite Index can also be included in other Market Bundles. For instance, Apple, Cisco Systems, Intel and Microsoft are included in the Dow and the S&P 500 in addition to the NASDAQ Composite.

While the three market indicators described above are the most prominent, there are many Market Bundles that slice and dice the US market to give snapshots of the performance of certain sectors. For example, the S&P MidCap 400 Index and the Russell 2000 Index track US mid-size and small companies, respectively.

Market Bundles serve several significant purposes. First, they are used as indicators of the financial health of the US economy as investors vote every day on the future prospects of prominent US companies. Second, the pervasiveness of the major market averages in the news is great marketing. Notwithstanding the fact that most do not understand what the Dow, S&P 500 and NASDAQ numbers represent, the big green and red arrows shown on TV get the public's attention. Third, and most importantly from the investor's perspective, Market Bundles facilitate the sale of investment products that mirror the performance of the averages: investors can buy bundles that replicate the relevant index, guaranteeing the return of the underlying group of stocks.

BUYING A BUNDLE

Both mutual funds and exchange traded funds bundle stocks based on a stated investment theme for the convenient purchase and sale by individual investors. Both offer portfolio diversification and transparency of holdings with positions disclosed at least quarterly. Both types of funds are liquid, meaning the investor can sell efficiently and obtain the cash proceeds in a few days. However, there are important differences between the two types of funds as discussed below.

MUTUAL FUNDS

Mutual fund bundles can be traded in two ways, directly with the investment firm sponsoring and managing the fund, such as Fidelity, Vanguard or T. Rowe Price, or through a full service or online broker. In either case, purchases and sales are made once each day at the close of trading. At the close, the fund establishes the value of its investments and calculates its Net Asset Value Per Share ("NAV"). The NAV is the price at which shares can be purchased or sold that day and is quoted daily in financial newspapers or on a financial web site, such as Yahoo Finance.

If purchased directly from the sponsor, the investor opens a stand-alone account that only holds the shares of that mutual fund (or shares of other mutual funds offered by the same sponsor). Generally, there is not a commission or fee for buying and selling directly.

If a mutual fund is purchased through a broker, the shares in the fund appear on the investor's monthly brokerage account statement. Typically, brokerage firms do not maintain relationships with every fund sponsor. As a result, the mutual fund bundles that can be purchased through a broker are typically less than the total universe. Importantly, buying and selling mutual funds through a broker can cost more as commissions and fees are higher. The investor should ask about fees associated with buying mutual funds from a broker -- the client is entitled to know exactly how much additional cost will be incurred. Be aware of these potential additional costs.

No matter which manner of purchase is used, investors would be wise to avoid a type of mutual fund called "Load Funds." Load Funds charge an upfront purchase fee (the "load") to the investor, sometimes as much as 5%. Often, all or a portion of this fee is to compensate a broker for selling the fund. "No Load Funds" do not charge an upfront fee and are generally a better deal for the investor.

When investing in mutual fund bundles, understanding the totality of fees, both upfront and ongoing, is critical. Since 1991, approximately 70% of all actively managed mutual funds failed to equal the profit performance of the S&P 500 Index and since 2006 the number failing is even higher at 85%. One of the main culprits for the underperformance of mutual funds is a high level of management fees and expenses.

Investors in stock mutual fund bundles are liable for their pro rata share of a fund's tax liability each year based on the fund's trading history. Each investor receives a tax statement from the fund that reports tax liability on a per share basis. This often results in a required tax payment for an individual who did not sell shares during the year. The investor can sell shares to pay the liability or pay the tax out of pocket. Many investors dislike this aspect of mutual fund investing.

EXCHANGE TRADED FUNDS

Exchange Traded Fund ("ETF") stock bundles are issued by an investment company, follow a stated investment objective, provide diversification and are required to report their holdings like mutual fund bundles.

Unlike mutual funds, the shares of ETFs are listed on a national exchange and trade continuously throughout the day based on supply and demand, like individual company stocks. ETFs can be purchased only through a broker with purchases typically incurring a brokerage commission and an additional cost drag from a market maker's bid/ask spread. ETF share prices approximate the NAV of the underlying portfolio, but continuous trading makes this a moving target.

ETF bundles can be sold short like individual stocks and can be used as collateral for a margin loan, unlike mutual funds.

First introduced in 1993, ETFs are a relatively new investment product. Since then, nearly two thousand ETFs have been introduced spanning a wide range of investment objectives beginning with passive, index tracking funds such as the SPDR S&P 500 Index ETF (ticker: SPY) and migrating in the last several years to more active investing strategies that follow a defined investment formula, sometimes referred to as "smart beta" funds.

An old Wall Street saying -- "money flows to its highest and best use" -- applies to ETFs. In recent years, investors have poured massive amounts of money into stock ETFs at the expense of stock mutual funds, particularly actively managed stock funds, because ETFs have performed better, making higher net profits for investors.

ETF bundles have trading advantages over mutual funds, but the primary reasons for the flood of money into these bundles are lower fees and lower current tax bills.

Total management fees for ETF bundles are lower than the typical actively managed mutual fund. ETFs operate at lower costs because they either track an index or follow a mathematical model with precise rules, eliminating the need for research analysts and stock pickers employed by actively managed funds.

I have seen estimates of the cost advantage of ETFs versus mutual funds ranging from a low of 0.25% per year to a high of 2.0% per year. Over time these savings translate into dramatic profit increases for the investor.

Tax bills are lower. Capital gains realized by a stock ETF do not flow through to the investor each year as they do in a mutual fund. An investor's capital gains tax payments are deferred until the investor actually sells shares of the ETF, giving control of the timing of tax liabilities to the shareholder. This deferral effectively acts as a perpetual, interest free loan from the government: the investor gets to use and profit from the government's money for as long as desired at no charge.

This tax advantage is particularly beneficial when investing in ETFs that buy and sell underlying shares to rebalance the portfolio quarterly or yearly. With these bundles, the investor gets a capital gains free rollover into a new portfolio at each rebalancing.

ETF bundles' lower fees and structural tax advantage puts significantly more money in the investor's pocket over time.

BUNDLE RULES

There are five rules of the road for investing in stock bundles. Violate them at your own expense.

1. Buy bundles to achieve diversification of a stock portfolio.

2. Invest in ETF bundles exclusively in taxable accounts. They put more money in your pocket.

3. If investing in a tax advantaged account, mutual fund bundles can be considered, particularly low cost index funds.

4. If an actively managed bundle is desired for a tax advantaged account, choose mutual funds that have low relative fees, a proven track record in good and bad markets, and do not attempt to approximate or shadow an index (called "high active share" in financial jargon). Examples of successful and efficient funds include Fidelity's Contrafund and Low Price Stock Fund and the Dodge & Cox Stock Fund.

5. Buy ETF bundles through online brokers. Buy mutual funds direct or without a fee to a broker.

3

Liquidity: Cash in Pocket

Financial liquidity is a measurement of how readily an asset can be converted into cash.

Assessing an asset's cash convertibility is based principally on two factors: time and cost. How long does it take for a certain investment type to be converted to cash in the bank? How much does the conversion process typically cost? Asset groups can be ranked based on liquidity characteristics, offering the investor a gauge of portfolio flexibility.

An advantage of investing in publicly traded securities (stocks and bonds) is the high liquidity factor. These assets can be turned into cash in a matter of days and typically for a minimal cost. In the case of publicly traded stocks, shareholders can sell their stock in minutes and receive cash on the settlement date (2 business days later, referred to as "trade date plus 2" or simply "T + 2").

Expenses involved in selling include the market maker's bid/ask spread and a brokerage commission. If selling a stock that trades hundreds of thousands or millions of shares per day, the bid/ask spread cost amounts to pennies per share. Trading through an online broker such as Fidelity or Charles Schwab currently costs $4.95 per stock trade. Full service brokers charge a higher commission.

As illustration, the total cost to sell 100 shares of a $50 stock through Fidelity with a $0.05 per share market maker's charge (100 x $0.05 = $5.00) is $9.95, approximately 0.2% of the $5,000 sale proceeds. Two business days later, $4,990.05 will be deposited in the investor's account.

Assets that are considered illiquid take a longer time to convert to cash and expenses are higher.

Privately held real estate, such as a home, is a good example of a relatively illiquid asset because cash conversion is a lengthy, costly process. A quick sale for a home would be 60 days from listing date to close of escrow (compared to the standard 2 business days for a public stock) and would incur brokerage and transaction fees of at least 5% of the sale price and often higher. The average sale time line for a home is 90 - 120 days. Such a transaction is longer and considerably more expensive per dollar than selling a publicly traded stock.

Within the category of publicly traded stocks, companies that trade more shares per day are considered more liquid than those that trade less. For example, approximately 75 million shares of Bank of America stock change hands daily as compared to approximately 980,000 shares per day for Ulta Beauty. Between the two, Bank of America would be deemed more liquid -- it is easier and cheaper to sell a position in Bank of America.

In theory, shares that are more liquid command a higher price in the market to reflect a lower level of risk to investors.

Part III – B

Bonds

1

You Are the Bank

The main alternative to investing in the stock market, in which the investor receives an ownership interest, is investing in publicly traded debt instruments, referred to as fixed income investments, commonly called bonds. When investing in bonds, the investor essentially buys a piece of a loan, acting as a lender and not an owner.

The primary attractiveness of fixed income investing is that the cash flows to be received by the investor are specified, or fixed, at the time the loan is issued pursuant to a legally binding loan contract between the borrower and investors. All terms are set in stone on the issuance date, including the amount of interest to be paid, the timing of such interest payments and the dates of principal repayments.* Absent payment default, the investor can anticipate accurately the timing and amount of cash to be received. Therefore, fixed income investing is less risky and has historically been less volatile than stock market investments.

In return for predictable cash flows, the investor gives up the financial upside inherent in ownership investments. Fixed income investors' profits are established at the time of purchase -- under

---

* Debt securities with floating rate or adjustable interest rates are sold and trade actively. While such securities periodically change the amount of interest paid, the changes are pursuant to a predetermined formula set at the time of issuance. Such debt instruments are still considered part of the fixed income market.

non-default conditions the investor will not receive a penny more or less than promised in the loan document.

Historically, fixed income investments have generated a lower total return than that of the stock market. Fixed income investors have been willing to accept lower total profits in exchange for a more predictable investment. Public company shareholders, receiving non-guaranteed dividends and uncertain upside appreciation, have historically been compensated more highly for additional risk and greater volatility.

ISSUERS

A wide range of entities issue publicly traded debt instruments, including sovereign countries, US states and local governments and foreign and domestic corporations. Sovereign governments, states and local governments sell debt securities to finance their day-to-day operations or to finance major public works projects. Corporations can choose to sell either debt instruments in the fixed income market or equity ownership interests in the public stock market to finance their businesses and capital spending projects.

The dollar value of fixed income securities trading in the US market in 2017 approximates $50 trillion, more than the total market value of the US stock market.

Unlike the typical public company that has only one class of stock trading in the public market, issuers can sell a variety of debt instruments with varying structures, maturity dates, interest rates and other terms. As illustration, if an investor is interested in owning a share of IBM, then he has one security and its quoted share price to consider. The fixed income investor interested in IBM debt securities may have 20 different debt instruments to choose from, each with varying terms.

Consequently, the fixed income investor has a dizzying array of potential investment choices.

To make sense of the market, it is helpful to categorize fixed income issuers into four groups: 1) Treasury securities sold by the United States government; 2) Corporate debt instruments sold by US companies; 3) Municipal securities sold by US states and local governments; and 4) Foreign debt instruments sold by non-US sovereign governments and foreign corporations.

US Treasury Securities: Debt securities issued by the United States government are referred to as "Treasuries." Treasuries are backed by the full credit and taxing authority of the US government. As such, Treasuries carry almost no risk of payment default. The interest paid on Treasuries, therefore, is referred to as the "risk free rate of return." The US Treasury sells three types of securities: bills, notes, and bonds.

Treasury Bills are issued for one year or less, are issued at a discount to face value and pay out at face value at maturity. The difference between the discounted price at which investors purchase the bills and the face value paid at maturity represents the income the investor earns for holding the Treasury bill.

Treasury debt instruments with a maturity of less than 10 years at issuance are called Notes and ones issued with maturities of 10 years or longer are called Bonds. Treasury Notes and Bonds typically pay interest twice yearly at six-month intervals.

US Corporates: US corporations issue all manner of fixed income securities from extremely short-term money market instruments like 30-day commercial paper to long-term bonds with maturities of up to 30 years (in rare instances even longer).

Companies can issue multiple types of fixed income debt instruments, allowing investors to choose among the different options.

In contrast to Treasuries, corporate debt securities carry a tangible risk of payment default. As discussed more fully below, corporate debt security issuances are rated by accredited credit rating agencies prior to initial sale to inform investors as to the quality of the issuer's credit and the issue's approximate level of default risk. Due to a higher risk of default than Treasury securities, corporate debt instruments typically pay a higher annual rate of interest than a Treasury security of comparable duration.

Municipal Bonds: Municipal Bonds or "munis" are issued by state and local governments. Like corporates, munis carry a risk of default and are rated by the credit rating agencies. The interest on most munis is exempt from Federal income tax and also from state and local income tax if the purchaser is a resident of the issuing state. Due to this tax advantage, munis typically pay a lower rate of interest than a comparably rated corporate bond of similar duration.

Foreign: Investors can buy fixed income securities issued by sovereign governments from almost every major country in the world. Those issued by Germany, the United Kingdom and Japan are considered nearly risk free, like Treasuries. The bonds of other countries with smaller or less developed economies carry more default risk. Argentina, for example, has defaulted on its government debt obligations several times.

Investors can also purchase debt securities issued by foreign domiciled companies. Like US corporates, these debt instruments come in a variety of structures, are typically rated by credit rating agencies and carry varying risks of payment default.

For US investors, investing in foreign fixed income securities carries the additional issue of currency risk. If the value of the local currency declines relative to the dollar over the life of the loan, the US investor's net gains will be impacted negatively. While most foreign debt is issued in local currencies, dollar denominated fixed income securities are available to investors.

THE PRICE OF BONDS

When first sold to investors, bonds are generally priced at face value, also called par value, which is usually $1,000. Bonds can be bought in multiples of $1,000 of face value.

After the initial sale to investors, publicly registered fixed income securities trade openly in the market and such securities can change hands at prices higher or lower than face value.

If a bond is trading at par, then it is quoted at 100, representing 100% of face value. If quoted at 105, then it is trading at 105% of face value. In order to buy a $1,000 face value bond, the investor will need to pay $1,050. If quoted at 90, then the bond with a face value of $1,000 is trading at $900.

INTEREST

The cash payments received by a lender from a borrower is called interest. Interest represents the cost of the loan proceeds to the borrower and income to the investor. Obviously, investors would like the highest amount of interest possible and borrowers want to pay the lowest amount possible. The balance of buy and sell orders for a particular debt issue in the fixed income market decides where these two competing desires intersect.

The dollar amount of interest payments on a bond is generally fixed at the time the bond is initially sold to investors. This amount to be paid is called the coupon and is quoted on an annual basis, called the coupon rate. For example, a bond with a 7% coupon rate pays $70 per year on a face amount of $1,000.

For corporate debt instruments and Treasuries with a duration beyond one year, interest payments are generally made twice per year. For a bond with a 7% coupon rate, the investor receives two payments of $35 every six months.

The table below shows the interest payments on a $1,000 bond at various coupon rates.

Coupon Rate	Annual Total	Biannual Payments
4%	$40	$20/$20
7%	$70	$35/$35
10%	$100	$50/$50

In the case of floating or adjustable rate debt instruments, the mechanism for determining the interest payment rate is established at the time of issuance, but actual interest payments vary.

The fixed income investor receives the coupon unless the issuer of the bond defaults and does not pay. Thus, credit risk is the fixed income investor's main concern: Will the borrower be able to live up to its contractual loan obligations?

If an investor buys a bond at the time of its initial sale to the public at par (face value) with a 7% coupon, then the investor's annual return is 7%. Assuming the note is held to its maturity date and the original loan principal is repaid, then the investor's total annual profit is $70 per bond or 7% per year in relation to the investment.

BOND PRICES FLUCTUATE

After the initial public sale, registered debt instruments can change hands between investors. The prices of these trades vary from par value as the issuer's credit standing and general fixed income market conditions change.

For example, if a company that was highly profitable at the time its bonds were sold begins to post operating losses, then it is likely the price of its bonds will decline and trade below par. The lower price reflects the fact that the issuer's credit risk has increased dramatically. Investors will only buy the bonds if they are compensated for the higher prevailing default risk.

Alternatively, if no change has occurred in the issuer's credit worthiness, but the general level of interest rates has changed significantly, then the prevailing price of a previously issued bond will likely differ from par value. If rates have declined dramatically, then it is likely that the price of the previously issued debt instrument has risen. In this case, the market is not demanding as high a rate of return and the bonds will trade at prices higher than par value. If prevailing interest rates have increased dramatically, then the bond is probably trading at a discount to its face value. This type of risk to bond prices is called market risk.

If the investor pays a price per bond that differs from par value and the issuer makes all contractual payments, then the actual annual rate of return the investor realizes from the bond will differ from the coupon rate. Fixed income investors refer to this as the coupon yield.

The price paid for the bond determines the ultimate rate of return or profit the investor realizes. This occurs because the investor buys the identical income stream (the interest payments) at differing cost prices, mathematically generating differing profit levels.

At a lower price than par, the bond generates a higher profit. The reverse holds true as well. If the bond price paid is higher than par, then the profit from coupon payments is lower relative to cost. Stated simply, buying an asset that generates $10 per year in cash for $90 will deliver a better profit than paying $110 for the same asset and its $10 yearly cash flow.

		Coupon Yield Assuming Purchase Price of:	
Coupon Rate	Coupon Amount	90	110
4%	$40	4.4%	3.6%
7%	$70	7.8%	6.4%
10%	$100	11.1%	9.1%

To determine the actual coupon yield to be received, the investor must know the coupon rate and the purchase price of the bond, including any commissions paid.

Bond prices move in the opposite direction from interest rates. Imagine a seesaw with prices on one end and rates on the other; as one side goes up, the other side goes down.

BOND PROFIT EQUATION: YIELD TO MATURITY

Paying prices for bonds higher or lower than face value presents an issue to fixed income investors that hold a bond to maturity because at the maturity date each bondholder receives face value for each bond regardless of what price was paid. If the investor paid less than face value, then a profit in addition to the annual coupon payments is realized. If the purchase price was higher than face value, then the investor incurs a capital loss. This situation is quite common -- prices paid for bonds frequently differ from par value.

The fixed income market uses a calculation referred to as "yield to maturity" to account for the difference in prices paid. Yield to maturity is a bond's contractually promised rate of profit to the investor in light of the actual price paid for a bond, assuming the issuer makes all scheduled payments.

The yield to maturity of a bond purchased at par is the coupon rate.

The yield to maturity of a bond purchased at prices lower or higher than par will consist of: the coupon yield (coupon rate divided by purchase price) plus a capital gain or loss (face value minus purchase price).

When purchasing a bond, the brokerage firm will calculate and quote the yield to maturity to the investor based on the price being discussed. Using a financial calculator, the investor can confirm the broker's calculations.

The investor without a financial calculator can make a ballpark estimate of the yield to maturity fairly easily. For illustration purposes, the yield to maturity calculation for a bond with a 7% coupon rate and 10 years until the redemption date is described below.

First, calculate the coupon yield. Assuming a purchase price of $90, the coupon yield is approximately 7.8%. ($7/$90 = .078 or 7.8%) For a purchase price of $110, the coupon yield is approximately 6.4%. ($7/$110 = .064 or 6.4%)

Next, determine the capital profit or loss on a per year basis. Assuming a purchase price of $90 and redemption at $100, the capital gain is $10, 11.1% of the investment. ($10/$90 = 0.111 or 11.1%) Assuming a $110 purchase price and redemption at $100, the investor incurs a $10 capital loss. ($10/$110 = 0.091 or 9.1%) Divide both results by the 10 years remaining until principal repayment to arrive at an estimate of the yearly impact. (11.1%/10 = a gain of 1.1% and 9.1%/10 = a loss of 0.9%)

Lastly, add the coupon yield to the annualized percentage capital gain or loss.

The yield to maturity calculation serves as the bond investor's profit expectation, assuming no defaults by the issuer.

	$90 Purchase Price	$110 Purchase Price
Coupon Yield	7.8%	6.4%
Capital Gain (Loss) Per Year:	1.1%	(0.9)%
Estimated Yield to Maturity	8.9%	5.5%

BOND RISK CONSIDERATIONS

The investor in publicly traded loans must take into account two principal risks: the credit worthiness of the issuer and the market risk associated with the general level of interest rates.

Credit Risk

Will the issuer of the debt security be able to make the payments specified in the loan document in full and on time? Answering this question is the essence of credit risk assessment.

While a seemingly straightforward question, begging for a yes or no response, the actual answer can be quite involved and speculative. Each issuer, be it a government or a corporation, has its own particular financial circumstances to take into account. Making things more involved, most issuers have many different types of debt instruments trading with varying financial terms, repayment schedules, maturities and restrictive covenants. How each new debt security fits into the issuer's overall financial picture is important to consider. Complicating things even further, all factors need to be considered in light of expectations for the future -- sometimes as much as 30 years into the future. How will the entity's financial condition and ability to make good on its debts evolve over time? As the nature of these considerations

102

suggest, the answer to the credit risk issue is rarely yes or no. A more qualified answer is required.

Financial firms called "ratings agencies" stepped into the breach to assist investors in answering the credit worthiness question. Beginning in the early 1900's, ratings agencies have issued a grade to each new debt security, evaluating the riskiness of an issue and following up with ratings changes as the issues trade in the secondary market. A number of reputable firms issue credit ratings, the biggest and most prominent of which are the Standard and Poor's Ratings Service ("S&P") and Moody's Investors Service ("Moody's").

These firms employ financial analysts that study the financial statements and prospects of issuers and assign a grade or rating to each security before it is first sold to investors. New fixed income issues carry at least one rating and, in many cases, two ratings from separate agencies.

After the security is sold, the rating agencies track the financial performance of the issuer and adjust their ratings as the credit worthiness of the borrower improves or declines. The objective of the rating is not to answer the credit risk question with a yes or no answer. The objective of the rating is to rank order credit risk on a relative basis to other issuers.

To do so, the agencies use a system consisting of letter grades to group issuers with similar credit characteristics. The ratings scales used by S&P and Moody's, as shown in the next table, are divided into two major categories, investment grade and speculative grade.

The bonds of investment grade credits are typically safe investments with very few instances historically of payment default.

For example, from 1981 to 2012, the default rates for debt securities rated AAA and AA where 0.0% and 0.2%, respectively, and all investment grade corporate bonds defaulted at a rate of 0.10% per year over the same period.

Bonds rated speculative grade, also referred to as high yield or junk bonds, carry a meaningful risk of default. From 1981 to 2012, the default rate for non-investment grade corporate bonds was 4.2% per year, with the lowest speculative grade defaulting at slightly over a 25% annual rate. A speculative credit rating is a warning to investors to tread carefully.

	S&P	Moody's
Investment Grade		
	AAA	Aaa
	AA	Aa
	A	A
	BBB	Baa
Speculative Grade		
	BB	Ba
	B	B
	CCC	Caa
	CC	Ca
	C	C

The more memorable labels we use in class to describe each grade are in the table shown on the right.

As these labels suggest, a AAA-rated bond is the highest quality bond then available in the market. However, the AAA-rating does not mean that the bond in question is guaranteed in terms of payment, only that of all the bonds in the market it has as good a chance of being repaid as any other. Payment defaults for AAA-rated debt are extremely rare.

For speculative grade bonds, it is important to note that a high risk of payment default exists and that it is the buyer's responsibility to investigate further before investing. High yield comes with high risk.

	S&P	Moody's
Investment Grade		
Best Quality Available	AAA	Aaa
Good Quality	AA	Aa
OK Quality	A	A
Low OK Quality	BBB	Baa
Buyer Beware Grade		
Best Junk - Homework Required	BB	Ba
	B	B
Average Junk - Step Carefully	CCC	Caa
	CC	Ca
Worst Junk - You Were Warned	C	C

An important result of the credit rating system is that the borrower's interest payments are determined to a large degree by its rating. For example, a AAA-rated corporate issuer typically pays a lower rate of interest than a comparable bond from a AA-rated issuer, a AA credit pays a lower interest rate than a single A credit, and so on down the tiers. As a group, investment grade debt generally pays lower interest rates than speculative grade issuers.

Speculative grade bonds pay higher rates of interest than investment grade bonds because their future results are less predictable, with a wider range of potential outcomes for the investor.

Market Risk

The quoted prices for bonds trading in the secondary market fluctuate above and below par. If you buy a bond, expect its quoted price and its value on your monthly brokerage statement to change over time. Often, the changes are quite small, but occasionally the price swings can be dramatic.

The profit of the fixed income investor who buys a bond and holds it to maturity is not affected by secondary market price swings between the purchase and repayment dates. Assuming no default, an investor's profit will be as predicted by the yield to maturity calculation performed at the time of initial purchase.

As discussed above, one reason bond prices fluctuate is credit risk -- the risk that a bond issuer's credit worthiness changes dramatically resulting in the issuer's credit rating being lowered. If a AA-rated issuer experiences a significant financial setback, then its bonds will likely be downgraded, perhaps to a single A credit. Since interest rates paid by single A credits are typically higher than rates paid by AA credits, traders will demand a higher yield from the now A-rated bonds than they did for the previously AA-rated bonds. When this happens, the quoted price of the bond in the secondary market falls.

Absent changes in an issuer's credit standing, bonds can still trade above and below face value. In fact, a bond with a maturity of more than a year or two is almost certain to trade above or below face value at some point as interest rates change in response to a variety of factors, including evolving economic fundamentals, geopolitical turmoil and altered inflation expectations. Interest rates also change due to basic supply and demand dynamics for the debt issue or issuer in question.

The mathematical relationship for bond prices is: as interest rates increase, bond prices fall, and as rates decrease, bond prices increase. The inverse effect that changing interest rates has on bond prices is referred to as market risk. This inverse relationship creates the seesaw effect discussed previously.

To better understand why rate changes affect prices of existing debt instruments, it is helpful to understand how bonds are priced when they are first sold to the public.

The yield for a new issue is principally established in relation to the then prevailing yield for the relevant maturity US Treasury security plus an amount to compensate investors for the higher risk of non-payment.*

As illustration, a AAA-rated US corporate issuer selling a 10 year note might need to pay a coupon 1.0% higher than the yield to maturity of the 10-year Treasury bond. This difference is called the "spread over Treasuries" and reflects the fact that investors demand a higher yield to buy the corporate bond versus the Treasury security. Assuming a 2.25% yield to maturity for the 10-year Treasury bond and a 1.0% spread, then the AAA corporate issuer would pay a 3.25% annual coupon.

---

* Buyers also compare yields to similarly rated corporate bonds.

The spread over Treasuries grows larger as the credit quality of the issuer declines -- the investor gets a higher coupon rate for assuming incrementally more risk.

For example, compared to the 1.0% spread over Treasuries for the AAA-rated corporate issuer, a AA-rated corporation might pay a 1.5% spread (3.75% coupon) and a single A-rated issuer might pay a spread of 1.75% (4.0% coupon). High yield or junk bond spreads would be larger still.

As Treasury rates change, investors change profit (yield to maturity) expectations from all fixed income debt issuers, requiring more or less yield from all issuers as the benchmark rates rise and fall. Remember, bond prices seesaw in the opposite direction of rates.

For example, if the 10-year Treasury yield rises to 2.5% one day later, then the just sold AAA-rated corporate issue with a 3.25% coupon would need to trade at a 3.50% yield to maturity (assuming a constant 1.0% spread over Treasuries). To achieve a 3.5% yield to maturity, the investor would have to pay a lower price than par, approximately 96.6 compared to a face value of 100.

Price changes resulting from market risk are greater the longer the time period before the bond's redemption date.

BOND PRICES FLUCTUATE LESS THAN STOCK PRICES

Bond prices typically fluctuate in a tighter range than stock prices. Contractually fixed cash flow (coupon payments) from debt securities permits a relatively accurate calculation of expected profits (yield to maturity) and intrinsic value of a debt security at the time of purchase. This compares to the significantly greater uncertainty of valuing future cash flows from stocks, which offer non-guaranteed dividends and lack an exact, quantifiable terminal value.

As a result, the standard deviation for bonds is substantially less than the standard deviation of stock market returns. The annual standard deviation of returns for short-term fixed income securities ranges between 3% and 5% and ranges between 6% and 8% for long-term bonds. This compares to an 18% annual standard deviation factor for the stock market.

Bond prices change, but not as much as stock prices.

TYPES OF BONDS

The fixed income market can be broken down into 4 major categories of issuers: United States Treasury securities, US corporate fixed income securities, municipal bonds and foreign debt instruments of sovereign countries and corporations. Within these four categories of issuers, there are many different types of securities an investor can choose from.

Debt instruments that the investor can purchase include Treasury Bills, Notes and Bonds, Treasury Inflation Protected Securities ("TIPS"), Secured Notes, Unsecured Notes, Floating Rate Notes, Debentures, Zero Coupon Bonds, Convertible Bonds, Commercial Paper, Certificates of Deposit ("CDs"), Repos, Collateral Trust Bonds, Mortgage Bonds, Collateralized Bond Obligations ("CBOs"), Collateralized Mortgage Obligations ("CMOs"), Collateralized Debt Obligations ("CDOs"), Equipment Trust Bonds, (Municipal) General Obligation Bonds, and (Municipal) Revenue Bonds just to name a few.

A recent search of the Fidelity online brokerage web site under the fixed income category came up with over 92,000 potential debt securities available for purchase, highlighting just how many options the investor has.

Do not worry if the above list and the over 92,000 potential choices make your head spin and eyes roll back in your head. Most have the same reaction. Fortunately, the individual investor does not need to be a certified financial analyst or fully comprehend all the terms of 92,000 fixed income securities to successfully invest in the bond market. The following sections on Buying Bonds and Bond Bundles will explain how to navigate these confusing waters.

Three fairly common debt types apart from straight debt (instruments with current cash interest payments set at the time of sale) are worth defining since they are often mentioned in the popular financial press. They are Floating Rate Note debt instruments, Zero Coupon securities and Convertible Bonds.

Floating Rate Notes: Floating Rate Notes are debt instruments that have provisions wherein the amount of interest to be paid is recalculated periodically (quarterly, semi-annually or annually) based on a formula established at the time of sale and set forth in the loan agreement.

The intent of a Floating Rate Note is to ensure that the (typically long-term) note trades like a short-term debt instrument -- at or very near to face value at all times. This type of note reduces principal risk due to changing interest rates (market risk), but still carries the credit risk of the issuer. These securities are of particular interest in a rising interest rate environment.

Zero Coupon Bonds: Zero Coupon Bonds are long-term debt instruments that are sold at a deep discount to face value, pay zero cash interest on an annual basis and are redeemed at 100% of face value at the maturity date. The investor's income, therefore, is the difference between the discounted price and the par value paid at maturity. The less paid per $100 of face value, the greater the yield to maturity to the investor.

For example, a 10-year Zero Coupon Bond priced to yield 8% would sell for approximately $46.32 per $100 of face value and one priced at a 4% yield to maturity would sell for approximately $67.56 per $100 of par. The investor who pays the discounted price, either $46.32 or $67.56 for each $100 worth of bonds in the example, would receive no cash interest at any time in 10 years and would receive $100 at the maturity date.

The Zero Coupon investor, by foregoing the receipt of cash interest payments, takes more risk -- both more credit risk and more market risk. As a result, Zero Coupon Bond prices are more volatile than comparably rated straight debt instruments, with prices fluctuating more as interest rates change.

The advantage of Zero Coupon debt is that the investor's annual compounded yield is set at the time of purchase and does not leave to chance the return on future cash interest payments. This type of debt security is particularly attractive when prevailing interest rates are at the high end of historical ranges.

A disadvantage of Zero Coupon Bonds is that an income tax liability is created by the amount of "assumed" interest the investor receives each year, even though no actual cash is received.

Convertible Bonds: Convertibles are bonds that allow the bond holder to convert the bond into another security of the issuer,

111

typically common stock, at a predetermined price using the bond as currency. Conversion prices are generally 20% - 30% higher than the prevailing market price of the company's common stock on the bond's issue date.

When converted, the Convertible Bond holder exchanges the face value of the bond for an amount of common stock, thereby giving up the contractually guaranteed income and redemption features of a fixed income security for the right to receive common stock dividends and to participate in the financial upside deriving from the common stock's appreciation. Generally, conversion occurs only after the price of the stock is well above the conversion price, ensuring a healthy profit in excess of the bond's yield to maturity for the investor.

Convertible Bonds offer the investor the safety of a bond with most of the upside of the underlying stock.

BUYING BONDS

The fixed income market is a dealer's market in which bonds offered for sale are listed by a securities firm. To buy individual fixed income instruments, the individual investor must contact a brokerage firm to explore alternatives.

When dealing with a full service brokerage firm, the financial advisor will question the client to determine investment objectives and to design the appropriate search parameters. The financial advisor will then contact the firm's fixed income trading desk to prepare a list of debt securities that meet the client's parameters that can be reviewed and purchased.

The process with an online brokerage firm, such as Fidelity or Charles Schwab, is slightly different. To buy a bond, the client is responsible for entering the search parameters into the system and choosing from the presented options. Specifically, the client logs on to his account, selects the "Make a Trade" icon and then selects the "Fixed Income" option. At that point, the investor chooses "Bonds" meaning individual debt securities or "Funds" meaning Bond Bundles -- mutual or exchange traded funds that invest only in fixed income securities.

From that point, the investor would keep narrowing the search parameters, focusing on type of issuer, credit rating, type of debt, and desired maturity. For example, one could refine the search to: US corporate debt, credits rated investment grade only, zero coupon bonds, and a 10-year maturity minimum. The search engine will then present a list of securities within those parameters to choose from with important terms such as current price, coupon rate, maturity date and yield to maturity listed for each.

I do not generally recommend that investors just getting started buy individual bonds for several reasons.

First, the terminology and all the acronyms can be more than a little confusing, leading to procrastination in the best case or complete neglect in the worst case. Second, debt securities typically require relatively high minimum purchase sizes. For example, US Treasury securities are purchased in $1,000 minimums and US corporates typically trade in $10,000 minimum sizes. For the investor just starting out or one that is contributing new cash each month and wants to continually allocate a portion of that cash to bonds, the minimums make the process difficult. Lastly, because of the minimums, achieving a diversified portfolio is expensive. Admittedly, the bond investor focusing on investment grade credits does not need the same level of diversification as the stock investor buying individual stocks, but some diversification is important, particularly when buying US or foreign corporates.

For these reasons, individuals interested in fixed income investments should focus on low cost Bond Bundles managed by reputable investment firms, offering diversification and low minimum purchase amounts.

2

Bond Bundles

Recall the dictionary definition of a bundle: a package of things wrapped together for convenience, often offered for sale at a package price.

As with stock bundles, Wall Street has created and sells bundles of fixed income investments for the convenience of investors, particularly individual investors. As a result, investors are not required to analyze the terms of individual loan securities and purchase them one by one to put money to work in the fixed income market. Purchasing a bond bundle provides the investor a diversified portfolio of fixed income securities within the parameters of each fund's investment objective.

Obviously, bond bundles fundamentally differ from stock bundles as to what each invests in. Structurally, however, bond bundles share many of the same characteristics as stock bundles, differing only in a couple of areas.

Like stock bundles, bond bundles are plentiful and available in both the mutual fund format and the exchange traded fund structure. The *Lipper Mutual Fund Quarterly,* published in *Barron's,* typically lists approximately 1,500 fixed income bundles using the mutual fund structure and hundreds more exchange traded fund products. Each has an alphabetic code, its ticker symbol, as an identifier.

Bond bundles are sold at affordable prices. The bundles trade at Net Asset Value ("NAV") if in the mutual fund format and at the market price per share, which approximates net asset value, if an exchange traded fund. The NAVs for mutual fund bundles are typically in the $10 - $15 range per share. ETF bond bundles' per share prices are typically somewhat higher. For example, of the 20 bond ETF bundles included in the Top 100 Exchange Traded Funds listed in *The Wall Street Journal* on November 24, 2017, the highest price was $127.15 for the iShares 20+ Year Treasury Bond ETF (ticker: TLT) and the lowest was $23.03 per share for the Power Shares Senior Loan ETF (ticker: BKLN). No matter what end of the price range, all are accessible.

For the individual fixed income investor, this is an extraordinarily good situation.

Owning a diversified debt bundle reduces overall portfolio risk by spreading credit exposure over a larger number of securities compared to a strategy of buying individual bonds.

The investor can buy a bundle focusing on almost any segment of the fixed income market or the total market. To do so, simply search your brokerage firm's database by area of interest -- US corporate high yield, for example -- and identify suitable bundle candidates focused on that segment of the market with a strong record of performance. If interested in the total market, the investor can purchase a bundle with a much broader investment mandate. The ability to efficiently and easily segment the market and also buy into the entire fixed income universe offers the investor great flexibility in designing a portfolio.

Since the per share prices of bond bundles are affordable, the investor does not need thousands of dollars to begin investing and can add money in small amounts efficiently.

Similar to stock bundles, bond bundles can be passively managed, mirroring an index, or actively managed where the fund's managers choose securities individually. As illustration, an investor interested in replicating the broad US investment grade fixed income market could purchase the iShares Core US Aggregate Bond ETF (ticker: AGG) that tracks the Bloomberg Barclays US Aggregate Index. Conversely, the investor could opt for an actively managed fund such as the Dodge & Cox Income mutual fund (ticker: DODIX) which has had an excellent track record of delivering attractive returns for investors over many years. Both have approximately $50 billion of fixed income assets under management at present.

Like all bundles, the annual fee paid to the manager of a bond bundle is an important factor to consider. As with stock bundles, passively managed funds are typically less expensive than actively managed funds and ETFs are typically cheaper than mutual funds. For example, the passive iShares ETF (ticker: AGG) mentioned above has a 0.06% annual expense ratio while the active Dodge & Cox Income Fund's expense ratio is currently 0.43% per annum. In all cases, comparing management cost -- in light of historical performance -- is a must for the investor.

Bond bundles differ structurally from stock bundles in two major respects.

First, because the majority of a bond bundle's profits derives from interest income as opposed to capital gains, the advantage of the capital gains deferral associated with stock ETFs is eliminated. Simply stated, mutual funds and ETFs investing in fixed income securities create almost identical tax implications for the investor.*

Second, active managers of bond bundles have done a good job of besting the performance of bond indexes. Morningstar reports that for the 10 years ending June 30, 2017, the median annual return of active managers is 4.83% (after fees) versus 4.48% for the Bloomberg Barclays US Aggregate Bond Index and 4.31% for the median passive bond manager. Morningstar also reports that 75% of active bond managers beat the relevant index in 2016.

This is substantially different from the performance of actively managed stock bundles, the majority of which have underperformed the S&P 500 Index over the last 10 years, after fees.

In competing with bond indexes, active bond managers have an advantage due to the way the bond indexes are constructed. Since bond indexes are weighted by the volume of debt outstanding, they tend to over-weight the largest and, in many cases, the more highly leveraged issuers. The issuers with the best credit standing and ability to pay or the securities with the best value characteristics tend to be underrepresented. This is not to suggest that the bond market is in-efficient, only that the indexes are constructed in a manner which creates a benchmarking opportunity for active bond managers.

Bond bundle managers also benefit from the ability to accurately estimate the future cash flows from their potential investments and to compare those cash flows to today's prices. Stock fund managers, with a wider range of potential outcomes, suffer from

---

* Since municipal bonds incorporate income tax advantages, a bond bundle focused solely on municipal debt securities would have income tax advantages over a bundle investing in non-tax advantaged debt instruments.

greater uncertainty over the timing of future cash flows. As a result, active management is more successful relative to the indexes in the bond world than in the stock universe.

Buying bond bundles is generally recommended for all but the largest and most financially sophisticated investors because the characteristics of bond bundles are very favorable to the individual investor. They are easy to identify and purchase. Investing successfully does not require sophisticated financial expertise. Bundles are priced affordably and a broad array of choices exist spanning the entire range of the fixed income investment universe. Fixed income active fund managers, as a group, have demonstrated a history of adding value.

The biggest negative to buying bond bundles is that owning a bundle exposes the investor to a slightly greater and more constant amount of market risk. Because net asset values of bond bundles fluctuate as interest rates fluctuate and funds are always investing (never in a complete buy and hold to maturity mode), a bond bundle's price has perpetual exposure to changing interest rates. Investors can manage around this issue by balancing bundles focused on shorter term securities (less exposure to interest rate risk) with bundles focused on longer term debt securities (more exposure to interest rate risk).

BOND BUNDLE RULES

1. The typical individual investor should purchase bond bundles rather than buying individual debt securities -- the advantages far outweigh the disadvantages.

2. Bond mutual funds and ETFs are suitable for both taxable and tax advantaged accounts.

3. When investing in bond bundles, go with a proven active fund manager. Superior past performance of active bond bundle managers (including fees charged) relative to indexes and passively managed funds is a fairly accurate gauge of future relative performance.

4. Minimize trading costs by buying bond ETFs through an online broker and bond mutual funds direct from the sponsor.

Part IV
Be an Owner

1

Get in the Green

Now is the time to learn how to get the cash in your capital account working -- earning enough investment profits to create wealth and increase purchasing power.

Having accomplished the hard part of the wealth creation process by accumulating cash to invest, make sure your cash is working effectively and that the investment proceeds stay in your pocket. Do not allow your capital to sit on the beach sipping margaritas -- with your broker -- while you are slaving away on the job every day.

INVESTING: GET IN THE GREEN

Capital account funds should be invested in stocks and bonds. These two asset classes have historically delivered profits in excess of inflation. Both involve increased principal risk as compared to bank savings or money market accounts, but the additional risk has been compensated for historically.

The most impactful way to communicate this important point is to look at the numbers. The following table shows what $10,000 invested in the major asset groups grows into over various time frames, using actual historical annual returns ("base rates") for each group from 1926 through 2009 and current rates for parking place accounts.

For comparison purposes, the table presents a 2.2% consumer price inflation hurdle rate. Investments above the hurdle rate create wealth and those below destroy wealth. The assumed 2.2% hurdle rate is lower than the 3.4% actual average yearly increase in consumer prices in the United States from the end of 1932 through 2016.*

While it is impossible to predict what future inflation will be, almost certainly $10,000 in the future will not buy what $10,000 buys today. The prudent wealth builder needs to invest accordingly.

In the table on the following page, investments that exceed the hurdle rate are presented in green ink. Those that produce less than the 2.2% inflation hurdle are in red.

As the red ink shows, the saver loses. Parking your money is a bad idea which gets worse as time passes -- the saver gets poorer and poorer.

Investors get in the green. Purchasing power increases and wealth builds because the annual rates of return from stocks and bonds exceed the assumed 2.2% inflation hurdle rate.

---

* Source: The Federal Reserve Bank of Minneapolis website.

GET IN THE GREEN

Asset Category	Base Rate[*]	$10,000 Invested at Base Rate[**]				
INVESTMENTS		10 Yrs.	20 Yrs.	30 Yrs.	40 Yrs.	50 Yrs.
US Stocks	9.6%	$25,000	$62,500	$156,400	$391,200	$978,400
US Corporate Bonds	5.7%	$17,400	$30,300	$52,800	$91,800	$159,900
US Treasuries						
Long-Term	5.4%	$16,900	$28,600	$48,400	$82,000	$138,700
Short-Term	4.0%	$14,800	$21,900	$32,400	$48,000	$71,100
Inflation Hurdle	2.2%	$12,400	$15,500	$19,200	$23,900	$29,700
PARKING PLACES						
Money Market Funds	1.0%	$11,000	$12,200	$13,500	$14,900	$16,400
Bank Savings	0.4%	$10,400	$10,800	$11,300	$11,700	$12,200

---

[*] Ilmanen, Antti. *Expected Returns*. 2011, Figure 3.1, page 39.
[**] Investment gains are reinvested and no trading costs or income tax effects are considered

The stock investor is the big winner, grabbing the most green. After 20 years the stock investor's account balance is more than double the bond investor's balance and has grown purchasing power by nearly 4 fold.

WILL STOCKS CONTINUE TO GRAB THE MOST GREEN?

Despite the ravages of the Great Depression, the OPEC oil embargo shock in the 1970's, the Internet stock price boom and dramatic bust, and the near meltdown of the financial system in 2008, US stocks have outperformed since 1926. The question for today's investor, however, is not what happened in the past, but what will happen in the future. Is it still a good bet to invest in stocks?

Purchasing public company shares provides no guarantees of profit to the investor: today's dividend is not contractually guaranteed and tomorrow's share price appreciation is uncertain. Bonds, in comparison, come with a written loan contract and precisely stipulated interest payments. As a result, equity investments are riskier and share prices are more volatile than bond investments.

Historically, investors have been compensated for taking on the additional risk and volatility of stocks in the United States -- 9.6% per year since 1926 versus 5.7% for US corporate bonds over the same time frame. This is not a uniquely US phenomenon. Equity investment returns around the world have exceeded that of bonds -- from 1900 to 2009 world equity markets delivered a 8.6% average annual return to stock investors.[*] While the

---

[*] Ilmanen, Antti. *Expected Returns. 2011,* Table 3.1, page 38.

precise profits and timing differ somewhat from country to country, the relationship between stocks and bonds is the same the world over. Stocks have earned more.

This relationship -- the equity premium -- needs to continue or the rational investor will not take on the additional risk of share ownership. If the equity premium disappears, stock markets around the world would likely crash and never recover. While economic shocks such as occurred in 2008 will undoubtedly recur, the complete collapse of the world's stock markets and economies is unlikely.

Many argue that at today's elevated valuation metrics, the US market will not deliver a 9.6% average return going forward. That may be true. However, the relevant question is, "Will the returns of stocks exceed that of bonds going forward?" Interestingly, while the US stock market is at the expensive end of the historical valuation range, the US bond market is even more expensive with interest rates near all time lows. The risk premium, which weighs the valuation between stocks and bonds, currently favors stocks over bonds.

In, *Stocks for the Long Run*, Jeremy J. Siegel, finance professor at The Wharton School at the University of Pennsylvania, provides compelling arguments that stocks will continue to outperform bonds. His conclusion is neatly summarized in the following statement: "There is overwhelming reason to believe stocks will remain the best investment for all those seeking steady, long-term gains."

If Professor Siegel is right, does this mean the investor should expect to average the 9.6% per year that stock investors experienced in the United States from 1926 through 2009? No. Stock profits will fluctuate from period to period. When the market is expensive, future profits will probably be lower. When it is cheap relative to historical valuation metrics, future returns will probably be higher. These relationships will play out over long time periods. In the short run, prices will move according to the forces of supply and demand. It is not unreasonable to expect stocks to deliver higher returns than bonds over long periods, but the exact level of those profits will only be known in hindsight.

Regardless of the level of future stock returns, it is a good idea to bet that the equity premium will persist. Thus, the best chance to build wealth is with stocks. Be an owner.

STOCKS AND BONDS WORK TOGETHER

Owning stocks is essential in a capital account designed for long-term wealth creation. However, many financial professionals recommend that some percentage of each account should be placed in historically lower yielding bonds or bond bundles to provide ballast and stability of values. Since bonds typically trade in a narrower range than stocks, allocating a percentage of a portfolio to bonds props up account values in times of bad equity markets.

While most financial advisors agree that the typical investor should have some bond ballast even in a wealth creating capital account, no consensus exists as to the "right" percentage split between the two. There are, however, three splits that are worth mentioning.

The first is that the stock percentage of a portfolio should be equal to 110 less the account owner's age. For example, a 20 year old would have 90% (110-20 = 90) of a capital account invested in stocks and 10% in bonds. A 60 year old would put 50% (110-60 = 50) in stocks and 50% in bonds. The theory is that the younger person has more time until retirement to recover from equity market drops than the 60 year old and the older person has a greater need for current income and account value stability.

Another is the 60/40 split. In this arrangement, 60% is put in stocks and 40% in bonds. I have not seen academic research on why this split makes numerical sense, but have seen analyses for different periods of time that calculated what such an allocation would have generated in profits. For example, from 1990 to 2009 it barely paid for US investors to take the additional risk and volatility of owning stocks: the US stock market gained 8.5% per year over the period while US Government bonds returned 6.8% annually and investment grade US corporate bonds gained 7.0% on average.[*] While stocks generated a slightly higher return, from a risk adjusted perspective bonds beat stocks. Those years were a very advantageous time for bonds as interest rates fell dramatically, ending in all time lows. Starting from today's low interest rates, above average performance of bonds is unlikely to repeat in the near term.

Lastly, one of the world's most famous and successful investors, Warren Buffett, has stated publicly that when he dies, the executor of his estate should put 90% of the estate in stocks, specifically a low-cost S&P 500 Index fund, and 10% in short-term bonds. I call this the Buffett Allocation.

After reading about allocation strategies, I have concluded that the allocation decision between stocks and bonds is a personal one. The investor's time horizon (both age and period before cash is needed) and emotional constitution are critical. If the money is truly intended to deliver long-term gains -- no matter what the

---

[*] Ilmanen, Antti. *Expected Returns*, Table 2.1, page 25. 2011.

investor's age -- a higher stock percentage is warranted. If the investor breaks out into a cold sweat when the stock market drops 10% or 20% or cannot sleep when their month-end statement shows a decline, then a lower percentage of stock ownership is appropriate.

As an aside, I believe that conventional wisdom on stock/bond allocation is influenced by the liability fears of investment advisors. Conventional advice seems to favor bonds disproportionately, almost as if advisors are more concerned about their near-term legal risk than the client's wealth creation. They would rather be safe (read: not sued by clients) than give the seemingly more aggressive advice, even though such advice would maximize the investor's gains.

My advice for my three children, ranging in age from 21 to 25, is that they invest 100% of their capital accounts in stocks. They do not have a near-term need for income, are most interested in wealth creation and have 40 years or more to recover from a market downdraft. In fact, they would be better off in the long run if a downdraft were to happen soon. They could then buy more stock at lower prices.

A few years ago, a friend asked for advice on this issue. By way of background, she was in her early 40s at the time, is a single mother, and has a high paying and stable job. She was interested in thoughts on how to allocate the capital in her Traditional IRA account -- by its nature a long-term investment vehicle. My advice to her was to use the Buffett Allocation: 90% stocks and 10% in a low cost bond fund investing in US investment grade corporate bonds.

Choose the equity allocation that best fits your individual circumstances and emotional make-up. Err on the side of a higher stock allocation, as over time the stock investor's account is worth considerably more. Note that the ride may be a bit rougher on the emotions as the percentage allocated to stocks rises.

INVEST. DO NOT DAY TRADE.

The typical individual investor should invest for the long- term, utilizing a fundamentally solid strategy through a diversified portfolio of stocks or an appropriate stock bundle. Unfortunately, this course of action is frequently not followed. Many misunderstand the stock market, believing that it is akin to gambling and that the goal is a quick profit on one or two high-flying, story stocks. Some even get a physical rush of dopamine just trading, regardless of outcome.

No matter how exciting or glamorous it is to be jumping frequently in and out of stocks, day trading is damaging to the wallet. Most individual traders underperform the market and pay excessive trading costs and taxes for the privilege. It is simply not logical to expect to trade more profitably than Wall Street professionals who have more information and get that information sooner, have lower trading costs, faster, more powerful information systems and control the order flow of trades to be executed.

Day traders delude themselves into thinking that they can beat the Street. Bad assumption. Day traders lose, particularly when the market makes one of its surprising short-term moves.

Individual investors are better served buying stocks with a long-term, ownership mentality. Remember, stocks represent ownership interests in companies and each share of stock conveys to the owner all the legal rights and economic privileges of ownership. The shareholder receives the benefit of a pro rata share of profits for as long as the stock is owned.

Know that public companies have to meet a rather high minimum quality standard to be able to register on an exchange and sell stock to the public. Public companies are not typically fly-by-night operations. Most have been in business for many years and have large, diversified operations. Owning a piece of an Apple, Google or Bank of America at the right price is an incredible opportunity.

Certainly, individual companies can and do go bankrupt when bad or unexpected things happen, such as the emergence of market disrupting technology or new competition, or even because of bad management.

Investors can maintain the benefits of ownership, but eliminate exposure to any one company by owning a stock bundle. Owning a fund that invests in the S&P 500 means that the individual investor is an owner of 500 large, successful US companies spanning the entire economy. Can one of these companies go belly up at some point? Certainly. Will a meaningful number do so at the same time? Highly unlikely.

It is important to remember these facts when market turbulence hits and prices fall suddenly. While today's price may be lower than yesterday's, the companies you own still employ real people working to make sales and turn a profit. If you own a broad-based US market bundle, take comfort in the fact that the largest economy in the world is chugging along.

Because stock prices are guaranteed to fluctuate, the individual must be mentally prepared for month-end account values to decline. It will happen. If the business (or businesses in the case

131

of a stock bundle) owned is still operating and operating satis-
factorily, the investor has not "lost money," only paper value
and can make that money back.

Stocks are not lottery tickets with a tiny probability of success
and a near-term expiration date. Shares represent ownership in
ongoing businesses. As the owner, you get the profits and dividends forever, no matter the price the market is currently putting
on the shares.

2

Ownership Strategies

The typical small investor should not manage a portfolio of individual stocks. Doing so properly requires a significant amount of effort and time, financial expertise and ongoing monitoring. Moreover, it is expensive to purchase the 30-35 companies required for proper portfolio diversification. Purchasing individual stocks without doing the proper analysis or by following the advice of your brother-in-law or only holding 3 or 4 companies are all recipes for disaster.

Purchasing stock bundles is the most efficient way to maintain long-term ownership positions in companies. With one easy purchase, the investor gets portfolio diversification -- a piece of many of stocks for one price. The investor also receives access to sophisticated strategies, receives these strategies generally at a low cost, and, if employing exchange traded funds, manages capital gains tax liabilities.

TOP 15%: BUY THE MARKET BUNDLE

To be in the top 15% of active professional money managers, simply buy a S&P 500 stock bundle. "The SPDR S&P 500 ETF (ticker: SPY) has outperformed over 85% of active managers over the last 3, 5 and 10-year periods."*

None of my students believe me when I give them this fact. They find it hard to believe that it is that easy to be successful employing such a simple strategy. They think it must be more complicated and difficult.

Notwithstanding their skepticism, it is true. Buying the SPY and receiving the S&P 500 return, minus a tiny annual fee, puts the investor in the top 15% of all active money mangers. This is the reason why billions and billions of dollars have poured into SPY in recent years, making it by far the largest exchange traded fund in terms of assets.

SPDR S&P 500 Exchange Traded Fund

Ticker Symbol:	SPY
Price Per Share (07/12/18):	$276.86
Portfolio:	Evolving group of 500 large US companies in 11 sectors of economy
Historical Annual Return:	+/- 10%
Volatility:	Standard deviation of +/- 15%; Delivered a positive annual return approximately 67% of the time
Expense Ratio:	0.09% annually
Tax Efficiency:	Excellent

---

* Advertisement for SPY. *Barron's* July 10, 2017, page 12.

New Portfolio:	As components of the S&P 500 Index are changed; generally on an annual basis
	Over 30 years, $10,000 becomes $174,500
Wealth Creation:	Creates wealth of $155,300 ($174,500 less $19,200 assuming 2.2% price inflation).

As the above data show, buying the SPY has historically been an outstanding wealth creating investment. SPY works because it is a consistent bet on the US economy -- always 100% invested in large US companies. While future profits will fluctuate and may not equal historical numbers, the investor is assured of receiving the market's performance.

SPY is simple to purchase and involves no additional effort to monitor. Open your capital account, enter buy SPY and hit send. Seconds later you will own a piece of 500 outstanding US companies.

Importantly, every year the SPY owner gets a slightly new portfolio without any effort or expense as components of the S&P 500 Index change, reflecting the evolution of the companies powering the US economy. Importantly, this rebalancing is accomplished without creating a capital gains tax liability for the investor.

TOP 10%: BEAT THE MARKET BUNDLES

Alternatively, if the investor desires to be more aggressive in an attempt to exceed the SPY's +/- 10% yearly return, there are several strategies that can be utilized. Each of the strategies discussed below have "won" versus the S&P 500 over the long-term and each have numerous real world and academic studies confirming the results.

The hard part in utilizing these approaches is that they do not win every year, only over extended periods of time. As a result, to use them effectively, the investor must be committed to a long-term strategy. Attempting to time periods of outperformance and be fully invested and sell when the timing is thought to be bad does not work. Accurately timing the markets has not proven feasible. Attempting to do so typically results in lower investment profits and incurs higher trading costs and taxes.

For each strategy, summary estimates of historical outperformance versus the S&P 500 are utilized herein, as time periods and research specifics differ from study to study. In addition, information is summarized as to the relative volatility of the strategy and the amount of time it has historically won or lost versus the S&P 500.

SMALLER IS BIGGER

Historically, a portfolio of medium and small public companies has generated higher returns than that of the big company dominated S&P 500 Index.

A good estimate of the long-term annualized upside of this strategy versus the S&P 500 is about 1%. Over 30 years, $10,000 invested at 11% versus the S&P 500's 10% generates approximately $228,900 versus $174,500; wealth is increased by approximately $54,400. This advantage is represented in the graphic on the following page.

Unfortunately, the superior performance happens inconsistently. The data in *What Works on Wall Street* shows that small stocks

outperform large stocks in approximately 55% of 1 and 3 year
periods -- essentially a coin flip.

SMALLER IS BIGGER ADVANTAGE

$10,000 Invested for 30 Years

Furthermore, the prices of smaller companies fluctuate more
than those of big companies. As a result, the performance of the
Smaller is Bigger strategy can lag the price performance of big
companies for long periods of time, putting significant mental
pressure on the investor during the lagging periods. Hence, this
strategy is difficult to employ consistently.

To use the **Smaller is Bigger** strategy most easily, the investor
can purchase one of three exchange traded bundles: the SPDR
S&P MidCap 400 ETF (ticker: MDY), the SPDR S&P Small
Cap 600 ETF (ticker: SLY) or the iShares Russell 2000 ETF
(ticker: IWM). Each of these operate in the same fashion as the
SPY, but are focused on different size companies. All three purchase the companies in the relevant index, re-balance as the
indexes change over time, provide tax efficiency and operate at a
low annual management fee.

The annualized performance of each compared to the SPY for the 10 years ended December 31, 2017 is listed below.[*]

	Annual Rate of Return	Improvement vs. SPY
SPY	8.6%	
MDY	9.8%	+1.2%
IWM	8.8%	+0.2%
SLY	10.6%	+2.0%

Smaller is Bigger works because smaller companies are systematically discounted relative to big companies. Investors pay a premium price for the lower volatility, greater liquidity and ease of trading that comes with large companies. If an investor can handle the stress of the more volatile smaller company universe, then **Smaller is Bigger** can create additional wealth over the long haul, as compared to investing in large companies alone.

PAY LESS, GET MORE

A stock investing strategy that has historically produced better profits than the SPY and better than **Smaller is Bigger** is **Pay Less, Get More**. **Pay Less, Get More** is my phrase for what Wall Street calls the "value" style of stock investing -- buying stocks that are cheap relative to the market or to a company's intrinsic value based on fundamental financial valuation measures.

---

[*] Source: Morgan Stanley Wealth Management ETF Research dated 3/01/2018.

Value versus Growth

For analysis purposes Wall Street groups all public companies into either value or growth camps based on valuation metrics. Lower than average ratios puts a company in the value camp. Higher than average places a company in the growth group.

Value investors seek out-of-favor or obscure companies that are selling too cheaply in the marketplace relative to long-term value, companies that have disappointed Wall Street, suffered a financial setback or are flying under investors' radar. Value investors take advantage of current difficulties to purchase shares at a bargain price. Value investors expect the companies to improve operating profitability or to be perceived better by the Street and thus to sell at higher prices in the future.

The opposite of the value style is "growth" investing. Growth investors look for companies with rapidly growing profits and do not mind paying higher than average multiples to own them. These enterprises are often perceived to be great companies, sometimes referred to as glamour stocks. Growth investors count on future profits growing rapidly to justify paying higher valuation multiples today.

As valuations of companies evolve, a company may be a value company at one point and a growth company at another. Apple is an excellent example of this migration. For many years it was a classic growth company, selling at a higher than market average valuation multiple. In recent years, Apple has been classified as a value stock as its valuation has been below that of the average public company.

My students relate to the slogan **Pay Less, Get More**, as it more understandably sums up value investing. The investor is looking to **Pay Less** -- get a bargain price -- expecting that the company purchased will revert to at least an average valuation multiple. When this reversion happens, the investor makes a healthy profit -- **Gets More** -- than the market bundle or higher priced growth stocks.

Value Produced Better Results

Historically, value strategies produced excellent investment profits, exceeding those of the S&P 500 and growth stocks.

To quantify the superior historical performance, I created a rough composite of the data contained in *Stocks for the Long Run, What Works on Wall Street* by James P. O'Shaughnessy, *Expected Returns* by Antti Ilmanen, and *Value Investing* by James Montier. Each sets forth data that confirm the relative outperformance of value investing, but cite varying studies covering different periods of time and geographic markets.

Creating a composite, as a result, is inexact and the numbers here should be considered ballpark estimates. While differing slightly in terms of quantification methodology, each of these investment professionals and many others agree without reservation that value investing followed in a disciplined fashion over the long-term is a winning strategy.

I estimate that pursuing **Pay Less, Get More** within the big company S&P 500 universe has delivered to the investor an additional 2% per year over the long-term.

PAY LESS, GET MORE ADVANTAGE

Large Company

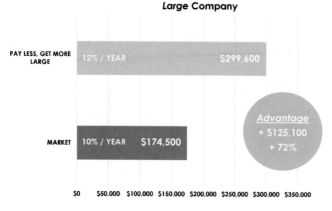

$10,000 Invested for 30 Years

Assuming a 10% return for the S&P 500, **Pay Less, Get More** generates a 12% profit per annum, creating significantly more wealth over long periods. Assuming $10,000 invested at 12% and 10% per annum for 30 years, **Pay Less, Get More** delivers $125,100 more ($299,600 versus $174,500) on the same $10,000 investment. See the previous chart.

Where **Pay Less, Get More** becomes really exciting is when applied to the smaller company universe. Here, the relative outperformance has been significantly higher, at about 4% more per year for the small company value strategy compared to the S&P 500. Assuming a 14% per year gain, the investor turns $10,000 into $509,500 in 30 years, creating extra wealth of $335,000 on the same $10,000 versus the S&P 500, as shown below.

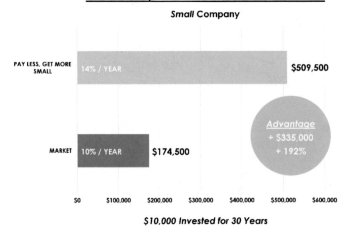

PAY LESS, GET MORE ADVANTAGE

Small Company

PAY LESS, GET MORE SMALL	14% / YEAR
	$509,500
	Advantage +$335,000 +192%
MARKET	10% / YEAR $174,500

$0 $100,000 $200,000 $300,000 $400,000 $500,000 $600,000

$10,000 Invested for 30 Years

Patience Is Critical

Pay Less, Get More does not win every year, but does win more frequently than **Smaller is Bigger**. For example, using price/earnings ratios as the valuation metric, the investor's odds of success -- beating the S&P 500 ETF -- are approximately 60% for one year periods, close to 70% for 3 year periods and in excess of 85% for periods longer than 7 years.

As illustration, one of my favorite US large company value stock bundles, Invesco's S&P 500 Pure Value ETF (ticker: RPV) beat the S&P 500 only 5 times in the 10 years concluding December 31, 2017 (a relatively poor ten years for value strategies). Despite winning in only 50% of the years, the investor in RPV who stayed the course generated a higher profit -- 10.0% versus 8.6% per year for RPV and SPY, respectively.

The biggest mistake individual investors make with value strategies is attempting to time the market: trying to be in value at the right time and out at the wrong time. This has proven nearly impossible to achieve.

BlackRock, a prominent investment firm, reported in December 2015 that typical value investors have not captured the full potential of the strategy. Their data shows that the average value investor achieves only about 56% of the available profit -- 44% of the gain is lost due to market timing. Losing 44% of the potential profit turns an excellent 12% a year strategy into a poor, market lagging 6.7% one.

RPV ADVANTAGE VS. SPY
10 Years Ended December 31, 2017 - Actual

$10,000 Investment

Patience is critical for investors employing value strategies. When markets are the hottest, value strategies typically lag, causing concern and the fear of missing out. Value investors do not often own the hot stocks or the newest technologies, but rather the boring, old technology type of companies or ones that recently disappointed Wall Street. These are not the stocks bragged about when standing around the office coffee machine. Remember, though, that the value investor makes a premium profit precisely because these out of favor companies are oversold and under appreciated. Waiting for this to change can test the patience of even the most seasoned investors.

How to Use **Pay Less, Get More**

The average individual interested in **Pay Less, Get More** should not attempt to pick individual stocks. Rather, individual investors should access value investing through a stock bundle.

There are many mutual funds and exchange traded funds that utilize the **Pay Less, Get More** strategy. The problem with choosing a value stock bundle is that no strict, uniform definition of the word "value" applies. All value funds are not the same. There are several guidelines to keep in mind when choosing an appropriate value fund.

If investing in an IRA or other tax advantaged account, both mutual funds and exchange traded funds are appropriate. If investing through a taxable brokerage account, then only consider ETFs because of their tax deferred capital gains treatment. As previously discussed, this effectively results in a free loan from Uncle Sam to invest.

In the mutual fund universe, the key considerations to apply to potential funds are: 1) Strong, historical commitment to and success with a value strategy; 2) Low portfolio turnover; 3) Low management fees; and 4) Managers with significant tenure.

Several funds that meet these criteria are: Dodge & Cox Stock and T. Rowe Price Value funds in the large company space; and Fidelity Low Price Fund and T. Rowe Price Small Cap Value in the mid cap/small cap universes. Performance data for these funds for the period ending December 31, 2017 is presented in the following table.

Value Mutual Fund Bundles[*]	10 Years
Large Company	
Dodge & Cox Stock	7.7%
T. Rowe Price Value	8.5%
Large Company Benchmark: SPY	8.6%
MidCap and Small Company	
Fidelity Low Price	9.1%
T. Rowe Price Small Cap Value	9.4%
Mid Cap and Small Benchmarks	
MDY	9.8%
IWM	8.8%

Excellent ETF options exist for investors seeking value strategies. Most value ETFs employ a more mechanical stock picking process, relying exclusively on quantifiable valuation ratios, than actively managed funds. Hence, understanding the selection criteria -- how deep into the value pond an ETF fishes and how many companies it owns -- is critical.

---

[*] Source: *Lipper Mutual Fund Quarterly published in Barron's* 1/08/2018.

Value ETF Bundles[*]	10 Years
Large Company	
S&P 500 Pure Value: RPV	**10.0%**
iShares S&P 500: IVE	6.8%
iShares Russell 1000 Value: IWD	7.1%
Vanguard Value: VTV	7.8%
Large Company Benchmark: SPY	8.6%
MidCap	
S&P MidCap 400 Pure Value: RFV	9.7%
iShares Russell MidCap Value: IWS	9.0%
Vanguard MidCap Value: VOE	**9.9%**
Benchmark: MDY	9.8%
Small Cap	
S&P Small Cap 600 Pure Value: RZV	**9.3%**
iShares Russell 2000 Value: IWN	8.1%
Vanguard Small Cap Value: VBR	**9.8%**
Benchmark: IWM	8.8%

---

[*] Source: *Morgan Stanley Wealth Management ETF Research.* March 1, 2018.

The table presents historical performance data for the 10 years ending December 31, 2017 for 7 large value factor ETFs included daily in the *Wall Street Journal's* posting of the largest 100 ETFs. All 7 are offered by Vanguard and iShares, two of the largest ETF providers. Also included are data for my favorite value ETFs, the three Pure Value offerings from Invesco.

As the data demonstrate, ETF value bundles compare favorably with mutual funds. It also shows that the Pure Value ETFs have delivered excellent performance.

GO WITH THE MO

Another investing strategy that has proven successful in delivering profits to investors in excess of the market bundles is called momentum investing. I refer to this as **Go With the Mo**.

Momentum investing strategies focus solely on the price performance of a company's stock, ignoring entirely its financial fundamentals and valuation metrics.

Using the momentum strategy, an investor measures the monthly changes in individual stock prices for the prior 6 - 12 months and compares those changes to the price performance of all other stocks in the market for the same time period to identify the ones with the strongest price momentum -- the stocks with the greatest percentage increase in price. Those with the strongest momentum are purchased and held until the next portfolio rebalance date. At each rebalance date the portfolio is reconstituted based on relative price momentum at that time.

For years, Wall Street traders believed in the benefits of relative price strength, but only recently has momentum investing been studied in a rigorous fashion.

147

In 1993, N. Jegadeesh and S. Titman published what has become recognized as the seminal work on momentum investing. Their article in *The Journal of Finance, Returns to Buying Winners and Selling Losers: Implications for Stock Market Efficiency,* laid the empirical groundwork substantiating the truth of Wall Street traders' belief in relative price strength. Jegadeesh and Titman, and others that followed and expanded on their work, have proven that following a strategy of investing in winning stocks works.

Note that since momentum investing depends solely on price momentum and ignores value investing's reliance on company valuation metrics, many think momentum and growth investing are the same. They are not. Momentum stocks are found in both the value and growth camps. The only factor that matters is the relative strength of the stock price, not high or low company valuations.

Following a well-executed momentum strategy has delivered profits superior to that of the S&P 500 and compares favorably to the returns of a well-executed value strategy.

In *Quantitative Momentum* by Wesley R. Gray and Jack R. Vogel, the historical performance of a generic momentum strategy is quantified. Their studies showed that following a generic momentum strategy from January 1927 through December 2014 would have produced a 15.56% annual profit versus 9.95% for the S&P 500, both before trading costs or tax implications.

Trading costs are a significant consideration for momentum investors as portfolios need to be rebalanced more frequently than the S&P 500 bundle and the typical value portfolio; Gray and Vogel suggest using a 2.4% trading cost factor to make comparisons realistic. Assuming a 2.4% trading cost factor, the generic momentum portfolio from 1927 through 2014 would have delivered approximately a 13.16% annual return versus the 9.95% of the S&P 500.

Based on the data in *Quantitative Momentum* and other research, I estimate that a well-structured momentum portfolio can produce about a 3% annual premium to the S&P 500 and about a 1% annual premium to a value portfolio. $10,000 invested in a momentum strategy at 13% per annum for 30 years becomes approximately $391,200 while the same amount invested in the S&P 500 at an assumed 10% becomes approximately $174,500. Therefore, the momentum premium puts about $216,700 more cash in pocket versus investing the same amount in the S&P 500 market bundle. See the chart on the this page for a graphical illustration of the advantage.

GO WITH THE MO ADVANTAGE

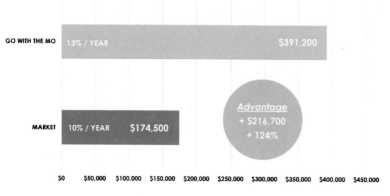

$10,000 Invested for 30 Years

Many attribute the momentum profit premium to investor psychology. Investors have proven slow to react sufficiently to good news from companies, exhibiting skepticism and a "show me" attitude. As a result of this initial under-reaction, stocks posting good news lag behind fair value for a period of time. It is only months later as investor skepticism is overcome that these companies get due credit. Eventually, the mispricing evaporates as valuations and stock prices head higher. At that point, the pricing discount disappears and future performance reverts to the pack.

As with **Smaller is Bigger** and **Pay Less, Get More**, momentum does not win versus the market bundle every year. However, if an investor is patient and stays the course over a complete cycle, the odds of success are quite high.

Just as there is no free lunch in life, there are a number of issues confronting investors with a desire to pursue a **Go With the Mo** strategy.

The first is volatility: the typical momentum portfolio is quite a bit more volatile than that of the market bundle and the typical value portfolio. Investors need to be aware that investing in momentum is a trade-off between the desire for higher profits and the reality of a wilder ride. If the prices of portfolio positions moving in greater, more violent swings than the broad market is a problem, then avoid momentum strategies. Patience and commitment are critical.

The next problem is a relative one: momentum strategies create higher capital gains taxes and trading costs compared to employing a buy and hold the market bundle strategy or a typical value strategy due to more frequent portfolio rebalancing. Higher tax liability and costs minimize the premium over the S&P 500 market bundle and also reduce the spread between momentum and value.

The last problem with **Go With the Mo** is calculation and time intensity. Stock prices for hundreds or even thousands of companies must be tracked, monthly averages calculated religiously and comparisons made to moving averages. For the non-professional investor, the intensity and financial sophistication required to execute the strategy is too much. Hence, momentum investing has been the exclusive province of professional traders for years -- until recently. The playing field changed dramatically with the 2007 introduction of the first momentum factor ETF -- the PowerShares DWA Momentum Portfolio ETF (ticker: PDP).

PDP solved two of the biggest problems the individual investor faces in using a momentum strategy. Investing in a professionally managed momentum ETF is easy and does not require any ongoing calculations or effort. The tax issue is solved by the ETF structure which creates a capital gains deferral for short-term momentum trades executed within the portfolio. The investor incurs no capital gains liability until ETF shares are sold. Unfortunately, high relative volatility is still a problem for all momentum investors, large or small.

Since PDP was introduced in 2007, the little guy interested in momentum investing has been able to invest like the most sophisticated Wall Street institutions.

After PDP, other US-focused momentum factor ETFs were established. Most notably, in 2013 the iShares Edge MSCI USA Momentum Factor ETF (ticker: MTUM) was introduced. Despite starting 6 years behind PDP, MTUM has become the largest momentum factor ETF with $5.9 billion in assets versus PDP's $1.6 billion at December 31, 2017, according to the *Lipper Mutual Fund Quarterly*.

As with value portfolios, all momentum ETFs do not use the exact same strategy. MTUM has proven to have an excellent structure, closely approximating the academic research on time series price momentum and focusing on momentum stocks at the lower end of the volatility spectrum. Importantly, MTUM is low cost, offered by iShares at a 0.15% annual expense ratio. These factors have contributed to its superior performance and investor money has flowed in at a prodigious rate.

Investing in a relative price strength strategy gives investors excellent odds of getting in the green -- ending up with more cash in your pocket compared to investing in a S&P 500 market bundle. As with value investing, bundle selection and investor patience are critical factors. In the case of momentum investing, commitment to the process and patience may be more critical because the strategy is inherently more volatile and tougher on the nerves.

BONUS BUNDLES: MARKET RETURN PLUS

An interesting twist on investing in the market index bundles, like the SPDR S&P 500 ETF, that has been a better deal for investors is what I refer to as **Bonus Bundles** or what Wall Street calls Equal Weight Indexing and Fundamental Indexing. Both have historically delivered higher profits with no increase in risk.

Index Construction: Before describing how **Bonus Bundles** beat the indexes, it is important to understand how virtually all the major indexes, such as the S&P 500, are constructed.[*]

The value of the indexes are the sum of the dollar market values of every company in the index. Each company's representation in the Index's total value is determined by its market value (called its market capitalization) with the result being that each

---

[*] The notable exception is the Dow Jones Industrial Average which is weighted by stock price.

company contributes a different amount to the total value of the index.

For example, at December 31, 2017 Apple had the largest market value of all the companies in the S&P 500 at approximately $869 billion. Compared to the total value of the S&P 500 of $23.9 trillion, Apple's percentage representation was 3.6% ($869 billion divided by $23.9 trillion) at that date. Another S&P 500 component, General Motors, with a market value of approximately $58 billion, represented a much smaller 0.24% of the Index.

As the prices of the 500 companies move up and down each trading day, the value of the S&P 500 Index moves up and down. The change in the price of the S&P 500 is the net difference in the aggregate dollar value of the 500 companies; the companies whose dollar value increased as their share prices went up minus the declining values as company share prices declined.

Bigger Companies Count for More: As a result of this market capitalization weighting, a change in the price of bigger companies has a greater impact on the total than a change in the price of the smaller components.

The following table shows the market values of the Top and Bottom 10 companies in the S&P 500 as at December 31, 2017 in billions of dollars: The Top 10 accounted for approximately 22% of the entire value of the S&P 500 and the Bottom 10 for only 0.22%.

S&P 500: Top and Bottom 10 by Market Value
(Dollars in Billions)

1. Apple $869	1. Signet Jewelers $3.4
2. Alphabet/Google 732	2. Patterson Companies 3.4
3. Microsoft 660	3. Chesapeake Energy 3.6
4. Amazon 564	4. Envision Healthcare 4.2
5. Facebook 513	5. Navient 4.2
6. Berkshire Hathaway 489	6. Range Resources 4.2
7. Johnson & Johnson 375	7. Trip Advisor 4.8
8. JP Morgan Chase 371	8. Under Armour 6.4
9. Exxon 354	9. Discovery Communications 8.8
10. Bank of America 308	10. News Corp 9.7
Total:	$5,235 billion	$52.7 billion
Percent of S&P 500:	21.90%	0.22%

Mathematically, an increase or decrease in the value of the Top 10 has a much bigger impact than a change in prices of the Bottom 10. For example, a 10% change in the Top Ten accounts for a 2.2% move in the Index while a 10% change for the Bottom 10 only alters the Index by 0.022%. In fact, the aggregate value of the Bottom 10 would have to increase by almost a factor of 10 (1000%) to have the same impact as a 10% move in the Top 10.

Expensive Companies Count for More: Another result of capitalization weighting is the relative over-weighting of companies with higher valuation multiples. Any company selling at a valuation ratio higher than that of the index as a whole contributes more index value than any company trading with a lower than market average multiple.

Assuming the S&P 500 Index has a price to earnings multiple of 18x, then any company selling at less than an 18x price-to-earnings ratio contributes less per dollar of earnings than any company selling for higher than an 18x price-to-earnings multiple. The result of this construction methodology is that companies at the value end of the spectrum contribute less than the companies at the growth end.

Amazon illustrates this point perfectly. At December 31, 2017, Amazon had a market value of approximately $564 billion and Wall Street analysts at that time were expecting Amazon to earn about $3.6 billion in net profits in 2018. This meant that Amazon was trading at approximately 154x expected profits, one of the highest valuations of the components of the S&P 500. At the same point, the entire S&P 500 was trading at about 18x estimated 2018 profits. Amazon was valued at nearly 9x more per dollar of earnings than the average S&P 500 component.

Valuations matter to the price of the indexes. The more highly a company is valued, the more it contributes to the index, and the lower a company's valuation, the less it counts. Well perceived, glamour companies like Amazon count for more of the total and the value end of the spectrum, with its despised companies, counts for less.

Outperformance Drivers of **Bonus Bundles**: The fact that larger companies and more expensive companies disproportionately impact the value of the S&P 500 Index creates the opportunity for different ownership configurations of the same companies to outperform the base index.

155

A. Equal Weight Indexing: Equal Weight Indexing allocates percentage ownership of a portfolio equally for each company in the index, regardless of size or valuation. If there are 50 companies in the index, then each company would account for a 2% position. If there are 100 companies, then each company would account for a 1% allocation.

In the case of the S&P 500 Index, each of the 500 companies would be set at an initial 0.2% portfolio ownership percentage. (100% divided by 500 = 0.2%) Under an equal weight scenario, the Top 10 which accounted for approximately 22% would contribute significantly less, only 2%. Conversely, the Bottom 10 would increase dramatically in contribution from 0.22% to 2.0%.

After the initial setting, ownership percentages change as company stock prices move up and down. Periodically, the portfolio would be reset or rebalanced back to the 0.2% setting for each company. At a rebalance point, shares of winners would be sold and losers purchased.

Since smaller companies (**Smaller is Bigger**) and value companies (**Pay Less, Get More**) have historically out-performed the S&P 500, owning higher percentages at these ends of the spectrum should drive an Equal Weight S&P 500 to better performance over the long-term than the base S&P 500 Index. This has proven to be the case.

In April 2003, Guggenheim Investments introduced its Equal Weight S&P 500 ETF (ticker: RSP) to invest in the S&P 500 on an equal weight basis. RSP has been quite successful, achieving a position in the *Wall Street Journal's* daily listing of the largest 100 ETFs with $14.8 billion invested as of December 31, 2017 and delivering better profits to investors than the SPY.

Since inception, the RSP has produced a total return per year of 11.5% versus the 9.8% of the SPY -- better by 1.7% per year. At those rates, $10,000 invested for 30 years would grow into $262,000 for the RSP and $165,200 for the SPY. The RSP places approximately 59% more dollars in the investor's pocket while investing in the same 500 companies.

With these types of real world performance numbers, it is surprising that RSP has not accumulated even more than its $14.8 billion in assets versus the $255.2 billion managed by SPY. One possible reason is that RSP does not win every year, in fact, winning in only 7 of the prior 12 years through 2017. This can be an issue for those focused on tracking the performance of the S&P 500.

RSP ADVANTAGE VS. SPY

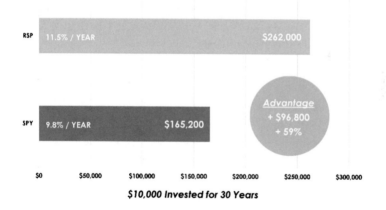

$10,000 Invested for 30 Years

Equal weight strategies work best when there is a wide variance between the largest companies and the smallest companies in the capitalization weighted index. They also work best when value strategies are working relative to growth strategies. Since both these strategies have outperformed over time, if the past is prelude, then the odds are in an investor's favor that an equal weight

S&P 500 strategy will outperform the base S&P 500 Index in the future.

B. Fundamental Indexation: Fundamental Indexation is a portfolio composition strategy that allocates ownership based on measures of economic production of the components of the index. Such financial measures are typically profits, dividends, book value and cash flow, but can include other production factors like sales and even research and development expenses.

Initial ownership weights are set based on the most recent production metric and adjusted at rebalance dates through analysis of subsequently disclosed financial information.

For example, in an earnings weighted portfolio a company with $5 billion of net income would be owned at a 10x higher percentage than a company with $500 million in earnings. In a dividend weighted portfolio, the company that paid out $2 billion to shareholders last year would be weighted at 10x that of a company that paid out $200 million.

Here too, academic research set the stage for the growth of fundamental indexation. *New Frontiers in Index Investing: An Examination of Fundamental Indexation* (*"New Frontiers"*), a research study on the topic of fundamental indexation by Jason C. Hsu and Carmen Campollo in the *Journal of Indexation* succinctly laid out the case in favor of fundamental indexation versus the market value weighting methodology used by most indexes.

The data in *New Frontiers* showed that over a 25-year period a fundamentally indexed portfolio handily beat the return of the relevant benchmark and did so with slightly lower volatility. In addition, the outperformance carried across size of company --

small, mid and large, persisted through economic cycles and occurred in each of the 23 countries studied. Interestingly,
fundamentally weighted portfolios outperformed in bull (up)
markets and did particularly well on a relative basis in bear
(down) markets. The strategy did not work in market conditions
in which price to earnings valuation multiples expanded iration-
ally, characterized as "bubble markets."

New Frontiers showed that a US focused fundamentally indexed
portfolio would have outperformed the MSCI US Index and the
S&P 500 by over 2% per year. An international, ex-US, focused
portfolio would have outperformed the MSCI World (ex-US)
benchmark index by even more, besting the index by over 3%
per year. Importantly, these results were accompanied by slightly
lower price volatility for the portfolio versus the index. The portfolios in the study used a composite factor weighting
methodology employing company sales, cash flow, book value
and dividends.

Premium yearly performance of 2% - 3% puts significantly more
green in the investor's pocket over time. $10,000 invested at 12%
and 13% compounds to $299,600 and $391,200 after 30 years
compared to $174,500 at 10%. Owning the same companies in a
fundamentally weighted configuration, the investor gains
$125,100 to $216,700 on the same $10,000 over 30 years with
no increase in risk. And since volatility is lower, the challenge to
the investor of enduring the emotional anguish associated with
dramatic market fluctuations is no worse than owning the index.

On December 19, 2005, the first fundamentally weighted fund
was brought to market, the PowerShares FTSE RAFI US 1000
Exchange Traded Fund (ticker: PRF). PRF uses a composite factor model similar to that used in the *New Frontiers* study: the
valuation metrics are sales, cash flow, book value and dividends.

From the introduction of PRF forward, fundamental indexation was more than an academic theory; it was being tested in the real world with real dollars.

	Annual Total Return[*]
	10 Years
PRF	**9.2%**
SPY	8.6%

In September 2006, PowerShares introduced a mid-cap and small company version of PRF employing the same composite valuation methodology, the PowerShares FTSE RAFI US 1500 Small-Mid ETF (ticker: PRFZ).

	Annual Total Return[*]
	10 Years
PRFZ	**10.6%**
MDY	9.8%
SPY	8.6%

PRFZ excludes the 1,000 largest US companies owned by PRF, owning US companies from 1,001 to 2,500 in size with portfolio weights determined by composite scores. It too has performed quite well over the prior 10 years as illustrated.

---

[*] Source: *Morgan Stanley Wealth Management ETF Research.*
March 1, 2018.

Other investment firms introduced fundamentally weighted ETF products, most notably Wisdom Tree Investments which offers an array of earnings and dividend weighted portfolios for US and foreign companies across the large, mid cap and small cap company universes, as well as currency hedged alternatives.

Worth mentioning is an old, somewhat famous fundamental indexation method called the "Dogs of the Dow" strategy. The Dogs strategy involves buying the 10 stocks with the highest dividend rates included in the Dow Jones Industrial Average (30 of the largest and most prestigious US companies) on an equal weight basis on December 31st of each year and holding them for one year. Each year, the portfolio is reconstituted, buying the 10 companies of the Dow 30 yielding the most at each December 31. The performance of the Dogs of the Dow has been outstanding.

What Works on Wall Street reported that the Dogs strategy beat the S&P 500 in 93% of the rolling 10-year periods from 1928 through 2009 and delivered an 11.2% compound annual return versus the 9.1% of the market over the same time frame. The data presented in *Stocks for the Long Run* confirms this conclusion, showing that from 1957 through 2012 the Dogs strategy delivered a 12.6% annual profit versus 10.1% for the S&P 500.

In class, we refer to the Dogs of the Dow and other fundamental indexation strategies as **Cash is King** strategies. Companies that deliver the most cash to shareholders or the most economic substance in terms of earnings, cash flow and book value -- not hopes and prayers for the future -- also deliver higher overall profits to investors.

Fundamental indexation has proven to work in the real world, putting more cash in the investor's pocket with similar volatility compared to a capitalization weighted portfolio, despite higher management costs. Fundamental Indexation strategies work by ignoring the hype about future prospects of stocks and owning more proven economic substance per dollar of investment. This approach is particularly powerful in regards to the smaller company universe where stories and hopes of future greatness abound.

INTERNATIONAL MARKETS

Historically, stock ownership in developed and emerging countries around the world has produced results for investors comparable to those of the US stock market -- profits well above the rate of inflation and better than bond returns. As the world economy grows -- with the US share shrinking -- and countries become more economically interdependent, it is important for US-based investors to include an international component in their portfolios.

Note that the stock investment strategies discussed in this section that have worked in the US market have also worked in international markets. Smaller international companies have delivered higher returns over time, but come with higher volatility and risk. International companies at the value end of the valuation spectrum have delivered higher profits than those at the growth end of the spectrum. Companies with strong intermediate-term price momentum have continued to deliver over the ensuing 6 to 12 months. Lastly, fundamental indexation has produced higher total returns with less risk than the base capitalization weighted indexes. As a result, US investors can apply the same guiding methodologies when looking for non-US investments.

Two aspects that make investing in world stock markets somewhat different than investing exclusively in US companies are the extent to which the performance of foreign stock markets are correlated with US markets and currency considerations.

If foreign stock markets were to move in the same direction and at the same time as US markets, then they would be said to be perfectly correlated, a correlation factor of 1.0. A correlation factor of -1.0 means that they had moved in exactly the opposite direction of one another. A factor of 0.0 means that there is no correlation between the two. According to *Stocks for the Long Run*, the markets of the EAFE group of countries (Europe, Australasia and the Far East) from 1970 to 2012 had a correlation factor of 0.65, which means that they have had some correlation, but have not moved at exactly the same time. The factor of 0.65 is enough below 1.0 that adding an international component to a US only stock portfolio provides diversification benefit.

Investors in international markets take another risk in addition to normal stock market risk, that of currency movements. Since shares in foreign stock markets are denominated typically in the currency of the host country, changes in the price of the host country's currency relative to the dollar will increase or decrease profits irrespective of the investment results.

Investors can choose to ignore currency risk, assuming that over-time the relative ups and downs will even out, or to purchase bundles that explicitly hedge currency risk. Hedging means that the bundle manager attempts to keep a constant relationship between the dollar and the host currency by buying and selling futures to lock in exchange rates. The cost of the hedging process acts as a drag on bundle profits.

A good guideline as to the hedging issue is: the longer the time horizon of the investment, the less attractive is hedging; the shorter the time horizon, then hedging makes more sense.

Most US investors should have an international component in their portfolios to benefit from future economic growth in Europe, Japan and other developed countries, as well as the dynamic economies of emerging countries such as China and India, and to achieve improved portfolio diversification. However, the average investor should not contemplate purchasing individual foreign stocks. Only invest in international stock bundles that follow our themes of **Smaller is Bigger**, **Pay Less, Get More**, **Go With the Mo** and **Cash is King**.

3

Red Alert

Investors need to understand the negative impact of fees on investment profits. While some fees and commissions are unavoidable, unnecessary fees can turn a superb "In the Green" strategy into a losing "Red Zone" one. Paying attention is the key to managing brokerage fees.

There are two basic account fee structures: 1) commission based in which fees are only paid on trades executed; and 2) a flat annual fee, calculated as a percentage of assets in the account, typically assessed and paid quarterly.

Online brokers Fidelity and Charles Schwab utilize the commission based structure for most accounts, with stock and ETF trades typically costing $4.95 per trade. Full service brokers are more likely to charge a flat annual fee. Generally, the fee is scaled to the dollar size of the account so that larger accounts pay a lower percentage and smaller accounts pay a higher percentage.

In commission-based structures, total annual fees will depend on the account owner's trading activity. Active traders will pay more than buy and hold investors. If the average investor follows the advice in this book and owns primarily stock bundles and holds for the long-term, the cheapest program is the commission-based program, executed through online brokers.

Being smart about fees can add up to very large dollars over long time frames.

The table that follows shows the impact of the two different fee structures on a $10,000 initial investment over varying time periods. The analysis assumes the money is invested in the "Buffet Allocation" -- a 90% allocation to large US stocks in the form of the SPDR S&P 500 ETF (ticker: SPY) and 10% allocated to a short-term bond fund. SPY is assumed to earn its historical 10% per annum profit and the bond fund is assumed to be focused on investment grade, corporate issuers and yield 3.5% per year.

Value of $10,000 Invested for:

Brokerage Program	10 Years	20 Years	30 Years
A. Commission Based*	$24,400	$59,700	$146,000
B. Annual Fee: 1.0%	$22,300	$49,700	$110,900
Drag from Flat Fee Plan	-$2,100	-$10,000	-$35,100
% Less than Commission Plan	-8.6%	-16.8%	-24.0%
Source of Fee Drag (Est.)			
Fee Paid	75%	50%	35%
Loss of Investment Profits on Fees Paid	25%	50%	65%

As the above table shows, the commission based program for the buy and hold, bundle investor executed through Fidelity or Charles Schwab is the best. Furthermore, the dollar advantage grows over time from $2,100 after 10 years to $38,200 after 30

---

* Assumes all the funds are spent in one purchase and a $4.95 fee is charged. The net invested is therefore only $9,995.05.

due to lost investment profits on fees previously paid. Said somewhat differently, your broker makes the money on the fees you paid and not you.

Remember the basic profit equation for investing: Investment Profits less Trading Costs and Fees less Taxes = Money in the Pocket.

All three elements of the profit equation need to be managed. Investing consistently and patiently in one or more of the market index beating strategies takes care of the first part. Using professionally managed stock bundles through online brokers or purchased directly works to minimize the drag from brokerage costs and maximize invested assets. Favoring ETFs over mutual funds, at least in taxable accounts, optimizes the tax element.

Stay in the green and out of the red by appropriately managing fees.

4

Do's and Don'ts

STOCK OWNERSHIP DO'S

1. GET STARTED: Get on the ownership train and start building a second source of income and wealth. Do not worry about timing -- now is always the best time to start improving your financial health. Do not worry about making a mistake -- the biggest mistake is not trying.

If you haven't already, open an account with Fidelity or Charles Schwab, the dominant online brokers with approximately 41% and 27% market shares in 2016, respectively.

If you have an existing account with a full service broker, request a performance review immediately. Ask for a year-by-year summary of the account's net investment returns, the fees paid to the broker, and what the appropriate benchmark returned over the same period for comparison purposes. If the profits are unacceptable or the fees are too high, make a change.

2. BUY STOCK BUNDLES: The typical investor should buy stock bundles and not individual stocks. Investors can choose from an unprecedented array of stock bundles executing strategies from the simple to the sophisticated. They are available to all, priced for convenient purchase, run by reputable investment firms and generally cost efficient.

These bundles offer proper diversification without any of the work or monitoring that come with investing in individual companies. Better still, the investor gets a new portfolio periodically with stock bundles which makes a long-term, buy and hold program feasible.

3. KEEP IT SIMPLE: Investing in stocks is a lot easier and more profitable than commonly thought. Most are surprised that the value of the S&P 500 has increased at about 10% per year on a compound basis since its inception in 1957.

There is no need to be a certified financial analyst or a chartered accountant to succeed. Nor do you need to sit in front of a computer screen all day to monitor your investments. Do not overcomplicate the mission: own companies.

Do not be put off by the confusing acronyms and jargon. If your financial advisor cannot explain a program in plain English and quantify why it makes sense, then run the other way.

4. CONTRIBUTE AND BUY REGULARLY: Add to your capital account monthly -- no matter what the amount -- and purchase additional ownership assets when there is enough cash on hand to offset brokerage commissions.

Do not worry about market timing. No one can predict when the market will move up or down. By purchasing consistently, the investor will accumulate positions when prices and valuations are low and when prices and valuations are high. The net result will be a fair price over time. This process is called dollar cost averaging.

5. RED ALERT -- BE AWARE OF FEES AND TAXES: It is not enough to focus on investments alone.

Every investor needs to know what account fees are being charged and for what types of assets. For example, there is no reason to pay a 1.0% annual fee to a full service broker for owning mutual funds or exchange traded funds that are already charging a management fee. Owning mutual funds directly or in an online account avoids these double fees -- increasing bottom line profits.

Know the tax efficiency of your account. Maximize the tax advantages of IRAs, 401(k)s and the like. For stock investments in taxable accounts, use the new technology of tax efficient exchange traded funds and avoid old technology mutual funds with their annual capital gains tax payments.

6. INVEST FOR THE LONG HAUL: While stock prices are volatile and future cash flows are not fixed like bonds, over the long-term the odds of making a profit greater than that from bonds and higher than the rate of inflation are quite high. According to Jeremy J. Siegel, "Although it might appear to be riskier to accumulate wealth in stocks rather than bonds, over long periods of time for the preservation of purchasing power precisely the opposite is true: the safest long-term investment has clearly been a diversified portfolio of equities."

7. BE PATIENT: The old saying "Rome was not built in a day" applies to stock investing. Do not be charmed by the latest hot story stock, hoping to get rich quick. The odds of success are low and the costs high. Rather, maintain a balanced, diversified portfolio of low-cost stock bundles and let the powerful economic forces of capitalism work.

STOCK OWNERSHIP DON'TS

1. DO NOT ASSUME: Do not assume that your financial advisor is doing a good job. Demand a yearly report outlining what your account produced and what you paid in fees to achieve the result.

On this point, I recently had an interesting experience. During the course of a visit from a family friend in her late 20's, we got on the subject of investing in stocks and bonds. She had little experience with the subject, but was very interested because she had a brokerage account with a fairly sizable balance. She wanted to know how to tell if her advisor was doing a good job. I suggested that she ask for a performance review.

After much back and forth, the advisor produced a well put together, professional looking report a few weeks later. It looked great, but the results were abysmal. For the prior 10 years, my friend had made an investment profit of 0.65% per year, net of fees paid, badly underperforming all the relevant benchmarks. Conversely, her financial advisor made 1.0% per year for each of those 10 years. It is not acceptable when the financial advisor makes more money than the account's owner.

2. DO NOT TRADE FREQUENTLY: Do not employ strategies that require frequent trades. Only brokerage houses and the tax man profit when you trade frequently. Moreover, do not even look at your account too frequently. Studies have shown that those who check their account values more frequently have lower investment profits than those who check less frequently.

In class, we joke that people "in the world" (outside the prison fence) should invest as if they were serving a 10-year prison sentence. The inmate's lack of smartphones, Internet, and financial information on companies, coupled with days old newspapers and the inability to trade regularly, results in the necessity of utilizing bundles with a buy and hold strategy. It just so happens that this is a pretty darn good wealth creating paradigm.

3. DO NOT USE DEBT: Do not use debt (margin loans) to purchase ownership interests. Using margin loans makes the broker a partner in your investments, incurs interest costs and adds additional complexity and worry. While perhaps overly conservative, a debt free portfolio provides maximum staying power in tough market conditions. To create wealth, the investor must be able to survive the inevitable market shock.

4. DO NOT CHANGE STRATEGIES FREQUENTLY: No investment strategy works 100% of the time. In fact, even the best investment styles are sometimes out of favor for long periods. Make peace with the fact that your strategies will not always earn the highest profits each year and stick with the program.

Part V
Never Sell

1

Portfolios

When we get to this point in class, the same question always gets asked. "All the statistics are great, but what do I do with my money?" What most want are specific directions: what to buy, where to buy it and in what quantities.

My only defense in boring them and the reader with the facts, figures and fundamentals is that any recommendations would not have resonated if the groundwork had not been laid. After exposure to the theories and data, you have the necessary information and knowledge to understand the answer. Understanding leads to commitment. Commitment guarantees success.

In the interest of providing specific direction, here are some easy to execute and powerful portfolio strategies.

BUFFET PLUS

As discussed previously, Warren Buffett, the legendary investor, has espoused what I call the Buffet Allocation -- 90% allocated to US stocks in the form of an S&P 500 Index fund and 10% to a short-term bond fund.

Pursuing the Buffett Allocation is easy: buy the SPDR S&P 500 Index ETF (ticker: SPY) and a bond fund. I would recommend the Dodge & Cox Income fund (ticker: DODIX), the Fidelity

Total Bond fund (ticker: FTBFX) or the Vanguard Intermediate-Term, Investment Grade Corporate Bond ETF (ticker: VCIT).

Interestingly, it is possible to beat the base Buffett Allocation. I realize that it is presumptuous to suggest a better investment scenario relative to the advice of one of the most successful equity investors of all time. However, in this instance, the facts speak for themselves. While staying consistent with the Buffett Allocation theme of investing in the large US companies included in the S&P 500 and without any additional effort, it is feasible to do better. I call it the **Buffett Plus** portfolio.

To get **Buffett Plus**: substitute either the Invesco S&P 500 Equal Weight ETF (ticker: RSP) or the Invesco FTSE RAFI US 1000 ETF (ticker: PRF) for the SPY. Both have bested the performance of the S&P 500 Index ETFs since their respective introductions. Keep the bond fund choice the same.

This slight tweak would have generated better net results historically and will probably continue to do so in the future. Both the RSP and PRF have outperformed because they have a slightly greater emphasis on smaller companies (**Smaller is Bigger**) and own more of companies at the value end of the spectrum (**Pay Less, Get More**).

The following table presents assumed rates of return for the SPY, the RSP and the PRF based on historical relationships, as well as a hypothetical bond fund yield. In addition, it shows the blended portfolio yield for each case assuming a 90% stock allocation and a 10% bond fund allocation, irrespective of rebalancing effects. RSP has historically exceeded the net return of SPY by more than 1% per year and PRF has won by about 0.5% per annum.

	Total Annual Return	Blended Yield Assuming a 10% Bond Allocation
Base		
S&P 500: SPY	10.0%	9.4%
Bond Yield	4.0%	
Buffet Plus		
RSP Case	11.0%	10.3%
PRF Case	10.5%	9.9%

To make the comparisons more concrete, the chart below shows what a $10,000 investment grows into after 30 years using the above rates of return.

	$10,000[*] Becomes	Buffet Plus Advantage	
RSP Case	$189,400	+28%	+$41,300
PRF Case	$167,500	+13%	+$19,400
Base Buffet	$148,100	--	--

---

[*] Assumes a $4.95 brokerage commission is paid, resulting in a net beginning investment of $9,995.05.

Opt for **Buffet Plus** to position your capital account to receive a return exceeding that of the base Buffett Allocation. Remember, the equity portion of **Buffett Plus** will not win every year versus S&P 500 Index funds.

CHEAP & STRONG

The **Cheap & Strong** equity portfolio consists of a 50% allocation to a deep value ETF and 50% to a momentum ETF. Periodically the two positions would be rebalanced to maintain the 50%/50% ratio. The investor can add a bond fund component to achieve a desired level of bond ballast.

Cheap & Strong is premised on the historical outperformance of value stocks (**Pay Less, Get More**) and stocks with strong price momentum (**Go With the Mo**).

What makes the combination work well is that the two styles have a relatively low performance correlation of 0.5 -- meaning the performance of the two correlates about half the time. While value and momentum strategies have independently outperformed the market indexes, both have suffered long periods of underperformance, severely testing the patience and commitment of investors. As a result of the 0.5 correlation factor, combining the two styles in one portfolio delivers both superior profits and shorter periods of underperformance.

I first became interested in combining the two styles after reading about the Trending Value Portfolio described in *What Works on Wall Street*. The Trending Value Portfolio uses a multi-factor screen to find deep value companies and then sorts those companies by relative price strength to end up with a portfolio of 25-50 companies. The profits of the Trending Value Portfolio as laid out in *What Works on Wall Street* were eye popping -- an 8% to

10% annual premium to the benchmark index. Plus, the volatility of the portfolio was less than the benchmark and the win rates were fantastic in 1, 3, 5, 7 and 10 year rolling periods.

For the individual investor, however, pursuing the Trending Value Portfolio presents two significant problems. First, arriving at the stocks to include in the portfolio is calculation intensive and requires a fair amount of financial savvy to compile and maintain. In addition, it is tax inefficient as the holdings in the portfolio change yearly.

Fortunately, I ran across *DIY Financial Advisor* by Wesley R. Gray and Jack R. Vogel which led me to two other books, *Quantitative Value* and *Quantitative Momentum*, and related published research papers penned by these two authors and T.E. Carlisle. These works examine how to combine value and momentum from a variety of perspectives.

The "aha moment" came when I realized that the solution was to purchase a deep value ETF and a properly structured momentum ETF and hold them side-by-side. In fact, the name **Cheap & Strong** was inspired by a suggested rule of thumb in *Quantitative Momentum* -- "Buy'em cheap; buy'em strong; and hold'em long."

To execute **Cheap & Strong**: buy the Invesco S&P 500 Pure Value ETF (ticker: RPV) and the iShares Edge MSCI USA Momentum Factor ETF (ticker: MTUM) in equal parts. Rebalance to a 50%/50% allocation periodically or as new money is invested.

The academic research suggests that the value/momentum combination should exceed the benchmark index by about 2.5% per year, 2% from the value side and 3% from the momentum side.

The blended portfolio should be more volatile than the index, but not as volatile as either style standing alone.

Over the period from 2014 through 2017, a 50% RPV and 50% MTUM portfolio delivered a 12.8% compound return (without rebalancing) versus the 9.1% of the SPY. The 3.7% annual out-performance was better than the academic research suggests, but it is a stretch to extrapolate that spread because the data reflect such a short time frame.

Assuming **Cheap & Strong** can maintain a 2.5% premium to an assumed 10% return for the SPY, over a 30 year period a $10,000 investment delivers $342,400 to the investor versus $174,500, improvement of $167,900 or 96% to the benchmark, as shown in the following graphic.

In the hopes of slightly better performance, investors can tweak this portfolio to get **Smaller is Bigger** into the mix by adding a smaller company value ETF, such as the Invesco S&P MidCap 400 Pure Value ETF (ticker: RFV).

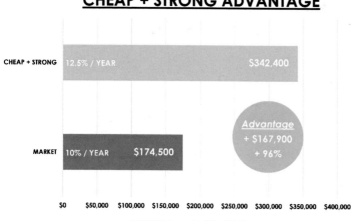

CHEAP + STRONG ADVANTAGE

CHEAP + STRONG — 12.5% / YEAR — $342,400

Advantage
+ $167,900
+ 96%

MARKET — 10% / YEAR — $174,500

$0 $50,000 $100,000 $150,000 $200,000 $250,000 $300,000 $350,000 $400,000

$10,000 Invested for 30 Years

BASES LOADED

Bases Loaded is an equity portfolio configured with 4 elements which incorporate all of the outperformance themes discussed above. By utilizing 2 broad market ETFs (RSP - large company and PRFZ-- mid/small company) alongside the more focused value and momentum elements comprising the **Cheap & Strong** portfolio, the investor touches all bases. **Bases Loaded** retains excellent profit potential and minimizes periods of underperformance.

Bases Loaded is summarized in the table below.

BASES LOADED

ETF	Category	Numbers of Companies*	Premium Theme	Portfolio Allocation	Estimated Premium vs. SPY
RSP	US Large Company	500	Equal Weight	15%	+1.00%
PRFZ	US Mid/Small Cap	1,408	Fundamental Indexation + Small/Mid Cap	25%	+2.00%
RPV	US Large Company	115	Deep Value	15%	+2.00%
RFV**	US MidCap	90	Deep Value + MidCap	15%	+2.00%
MTUM	US Large/MidCap	125	Momentum	30%	+3.00%
Total				100%	+2.15%

---

* As of December 31, 2017.
** Theoretically, RFV should deliver a higher return over time than RPV. The simplifying assumption made above is that the two are equal.

180

With an estimated 2.15% annual profit premium to SPY, this portfolio would deliver $311,900 to the investor after 30 years versus the $174,500 from SPY and should suffer shorter periods of underperformance than **Cheap & Strong**.

GLOBETROTTER

Adding an international equity component to a long-term stock ownership program can be beneficial.

Owning the S&P 500 offers the investor exposure to international economies as most of the large, US domiciled companies included in the S&P 500 transact significant business around the world. Adding more international exposure than just the S&P 500 to a stock portfolio should increase returns slightly and risk should decrease a tad as the US and world stock markets' similar profit levels are not perfectly correlated.

To add an international component, the investor adds one or more ETF bundles focused on investing in companies headquartered outside the United States to one of the US-focused portfolios discussed above (**Buffet Plus, Cheap & Strong or Bases Loaded**) and rebalance periodically.

The investor needs to decide what percentage of a total stock allocation to dedicate to international bundles and then adjust the US portion accordingly. For example, if the investor chooses a 30% allocation to international stocks, then the US stock portion would equal 70% of the stock allocation. No change is required to bond allocations.

As illustration, in the case of a 30% international allocation and assuming the **Buffet Plus** portfolio as the US base, RSP would account for 63% of the stock portfolio (0.7 US x 90% stock =

63%) and the international bundle(s) would equal 27% (0.3 international x 90% stock = 27%) for a total of 90% of the portfolio's dollars. The bond component would be constant at 10% of the total.

For one stop shopping, the investor can purchase a broad market, capitalization weighted market bundle such as the Vanguard FTSE All-World (Ex-US) ETF (ticker: VEU) which owns companies of all sizes from markets around the world. Alternatively, the investor can opt for a market capitalization weighted ETF focused solely on developed economy markets, such as the iShares MSCI EAFE ETF (ticker: EFA), or can invest in the emerging markets, receiving exposure to rapidly growing economies such as China, India and Brazil, by purchasing the iShares MSCI Emerging Markets ETF (ticker: EEM). All are priced in dollars and trade on US exchanges.

The investor also has the option of purchasing ETFs that focus on the stock market of a single country.

The international investor should follow proven outperformance themes when adding international bundles. Favor bundles using **Smaller is Bigger** (smaller company premium), **Pay Less, Get More** (value premium), **Go With the Mo** (relative price strength premium), **Equal Weight** indexation (smaller company and value tilt), and **Fundamental Indexation** (fundamental value tilt).

One suggested international portfolio configuration consists of two ETFs offered by Invesco that employ a **Fundamental Indexation** strategy (weighting by sales, cash flow, book value and dividends) across developed market economies in combination with a dividend weighted ETF targeting the emerging markets.

The Invesco FTSE RAFI Developed Markets (Ex-US) ETF (ticker: PXF) purchases large capitalization companies and the Invesco FTSE RAFI Developed Markets (EX-US) Small-Mid ETF (ticker: PDN) owns small and midcap entities. Both utilize the same fundamental indexation weighting methodology as the US-focused PRF and PRFZ and both have performed well since introduction in 2007, beating the return of the capitalization weighted VEU and EFA bundles mentioned above.

Purchasing the Wisdom Tree Emerging Markets High Dividend ETF (ticker: DEM) offers participation in the markets of the emerging economies of the world but in a conservative, dividend weighted format. Since its introduction in 2007, DEM has bested the return of the MSCI Emerging Markets Index ETF (ticker: EEM).

The following table configures a sample **Globetrotter** portfolio assuming a 30% international allocation and using the **Cheap & Strong** strategy as the US base.

GLOBETROTTER

ETF	Percent Allocation	Investment Theme
US		
RPV	35.0%	Deep Value
MTUM	35.0%	Price Momentum
Total US	70.0%	
International		
PXF	10.0%	Developed Markets, Large, Fundamentally Indexed
PDN	10.0%	Developed Markets, Small/MidCap, Fundamentally Indexed
DEM	10.0%	Emerging Markets, Dividend Weighted
Total International	30.0%	
Total Stock	100.0%	

2

Portfolio Management

RED ALERT: BUNDLES ARE BORING

Investing in stock bundles is the best way for the average person to own stocks and receive the significant, long-term wealth creating benefits of company ownership. As good as bundle investing is, however, I hear one complaint over and over, "Buying stock bundles is boring."

The reality is that owning stock bundles is just not as fun as owning individual names. Most relate to buying shares of Google, Snap, Bank of America or Krispy Kreme Doughnuts a lot more than they do to buying the Invesco Pure Value S&P 500 ETF or the FTSE RAFI US 1500 Small-Mid ETF. Not only are these ETF names tongue twisters, but owning a portfolio of 500 or 1000 companies is just not as sexy and interesting as purchasing the next Amazon or Microsoft. This is particularly true when the market is rising and a friend mentions how his "next Microsoft" is up 50% and your ETF is only up 20%. Never forget that the same person never mentions his "next Microsoft" when it declines 75% or files for bankruptcy becoming the next Pets.com.

The solution for the investor who desires to own individual stocks is to allocate a small percentage (5%-10%) of a stock portfolio to what I refer to as "speculative names." This will add some excitement and fun to the portfolio. Even with the

185

speculative names, the investor should utilize a value or a relative price strength strategy to identify good candidates. Do not simply listen to your co-worker or brother-in-law when buying stocks (unless your co-worker or brother-in-law is Warren Buffett or Will Danoff). Do some research -- know what you own. Have a point of view -- know why you own it. Invest -- do not day trade.

REBALANCING

Investing in rules based ETF bundles is the ultimate buy and hold stock strategy; the investor does virtually nothing after purchasing an ETF. As discussed, combining stock bundles that have similar long-term profit characteristics and risk but imperfect correlation between them increases returns and decreases risk.

Since all equity investment strategies, even the best ones, do not work at the exact same time, when one strategy or segment of the market has outperformed or underperformed, allocations can become unbalanced within a portfolio. Rebalancing allows the investor to optimize the benefit of combining strategies with imperfect correlations.

As a result, it is recommended that portfolios are rebalanced periodically to maintain desired allocations. Doing so takes advantage of the strong tendency of stock market strategies to revert to their respective long-term base rates and risk levels (called reversion to the mean).

For example, if small company stocks as a group have underperformed large company stocks for an extended period, then it is likely that the situation will reverse in the future. The easiest way to think of this process is to think of selling the "overpriced and expensive" and buying the "underpriced and inexpensive."

I have had students correctly comment that this advice flies in the face of the Wall Street truism to "let winners run and sell losers." Understand that rebalancing works best when it is applied to categories of stocks (i.e. small company versus large or value versus growth) and not to individual company stocks which have dynamics unique to their own circumstances.

For a concrete example of how rebalancing works, let's assume an investor is employing the **Cheap & Strong** portfolio. **Cheap & Strong** consists of two ETFs: 50% is a high conviction value bundle and the other half is an ETF bundle employing a relative price momentum strategy. Further assume that for three years consecutively value has out-performed momentum so that the value "half" represents 70% of the dollars in the stock portfolio and the momentum "half" only accounts for 30%.

At this point, the investor sells shares of the value ETF and buys more shares of the momentum bundle until the dollars allocated to each ETF are again equal. If the value strategy has outperformed the momentum portion for a long period of time, then it is likely to underperform momentum for a period going forward. Balancing the dollars back to 50%/50% permits the investor to maximize the combined benefit of the two strategies.

Portfolio rebalancing decisions require consideration of timing and taxes. Since selling ETF bundle shares incurs trading costs and creates a capital gains tax event in taxable accounts, how often should one rebalance?

In general, consider rebalancing taxable accounts every two to three years or when one component of the portfolio massively

187

underperforms or overperforms. Tax advantaged accounts, such as IRAs, can be rebalanced more frequently as selling does not create an immediate tax liability.

A cost-efficient way to maintain balance in a portfolio is what I call the "new money" allocation system. Using the new money system, new funds deposited or cash dividends received in the account go to purchasing the underperforming strategy, continually maintaining the required balance.

The "new money" rebalancing program is particularly applicable for those early in the wealth building process or when performance differences between positions are relatively minor. Using new money rebalancing reduces or eliminates the need to sell shares, minimizing trading costs and efficiently managing tax liabilities

DIVIDEND REINVESTMENT

Investors can choose to have cash dividends and distributions received from most stocks, exchange traded funds and mutual funds automatically reinvested in additional shares. Fidelity and Charles Schwab execute this service at no charge. Full service brokers have been known to charge a fee. For example, Edward Jones charges a 2.0% fee for dividends reinvested.

Automatically reinvesting dividends is an easy and efficient way to get small dollar amounts immediately reinvested.

PROFIT MEASUREMENT

Over the years teaching investment classes, one issue has repeatedly confused everyone -- calculating investment profits.

One would think that brokerage firms' monthly account statements would make arriving at profit numbers simple and straightforward. They do not. They are exceptionally good at tracking money flows into and out of accounts and informing the investor of the total value of an account at month-end or year-end. The typical brokerage statement does a poor job of allowing the investor to easily assess the profitability of individual positions relative to cash invested.

The confusion centers on how new money deposited into the brokerage account is presented.

Essentially, there are two types of cash money deposited in brokerage accounts. The first is cash deposited by the account holder that is used to purchase securities ("Deposits"). The second is cash received from existing investments in the form of interest received on bonds, dividends from stocks and exchange traded funds, and distributions from mutual funds ("Realized Income"). Distinguishing between the two is important as only Realized Income counts as investment gains. Many wrongly equate Deposits with investment profits.

Looking at an example helps to distinguish between the two. Assume a capital account has a value of $10,000 at the beginning of the year and has increased through December 30th to a total value of $11,000 without the benefit of any new Deposits by the account owner. In this case, the $1,000 increase in value is investment profit, as shown below.

Account Value on January 1, 2017:	$10,000
Deposits:	None
Account Value on December 30, 2017:	$11,000
Percent Increase:	10%

Since no new cash was deposited into the account from January 1st through December 30th, the investment gain was 10% of the beginning account value.

Now, assume that a $1,500 deposit was made by the account owner on December 31, 2017 and that the account's value at that date was $12,500.

Account Value on December 30, 2017:	$11,000
Deposit on December 31, 2017:	$ 1,500
Account Value on December 31, 2017:	$12,500

While the value of the account increased by 25% from the beginning of the year ($2,500 increase in value/$10,000 beginning balance = 25%), only 10% of that is investment profit and 15% is from the Deposit on December 31.

Realized Income: Realized Income is the cash that is received from an account's existing securities positions, irrespective of Deposits by the account owner.

In the case of stocks and exchange traded funds, the most common is income from quarterly dividends. Investors can choose to have these dividends paid in cash or have them automatically reinvested in additional shares of the entity issuing the dividend. Confusion relative to profit measurement arises from both treatments.

When dividends and distributions are taken in cash, the amount of the dividend is placed in the account's cash balance. The problem is that future reporting does not reference amounts previously paid by the respective company or fund. New investors often forget about these dividends when estimating the historical profitability of a position.

During a recent visit, a friend brought up this very issue. We were discussing investments generally and he mentioned that about 5 years ago he bought some stock in Pfizer, the large multi-national pharmaceutical company (ticker: PFE). He invested $12,800 which translated into a cost of $25.60 per share. His brokerage statement for December 2017 listed the value of his 500 shares as $18,110, $36.22 per share. The statement further showed that he had a gain of 41.5%. He calculated that he had made a little over 8% per year on his position in PFE (41.5%/5 years = 8.3% per year).

He was thinking about selling the Pfizer position because the stock's price gain lagged the broader market. I remembered that Pfizer was one of the high yielding Dogs of the Dow stocks and asked whether he factored into his calculations the dividends PFE paid. He had not.

After gathering the information, it turned out that over his five-year holding period PFE had paid out a total of $5.60 per share in dividends, averaging 4.4% per year on his original cost. Including these dividends in his profit calculation, he came up with a gain of about 12.7% per year and was no longer thinking about dumping his PFE shares.

Make sure to include cash dividends paid when calculating total profits from a stock or exchange traded fund position. Finding this information may take a little digging.

When investors choose to have dividends automatically reinvested, another accounting treatment occurs that is confusing. The confusion happens because the dollar amount of dividends reinvested is added to the cost of the original position resulting in a rising cost figure on the monthly statement. This occurs despite the fact that the investor has not come out-of pocket with cash to purchase new shares.

To illustrate this point, let's take my friend's Pfizer investment and assume dividends had been reinvested in additional PFE shares. The following table shows how dividend reinvestment would have worked relative to his 500 shares of PFE. For simplicity, the data in the table assumes that the year's dividend is paid out and reinvested only once a year. The table also assumes a hypothetical price for PFE stock on the reinvestment date.

PFIZER: 500 Shares Owned

Date	Dividend Paid Per Share	Dollar Amount	Assumed Stock Price*	Aggregate Cost	Shares Owned
Initial Purchase				$12,800	500.0
Year 1	$0.96	$480	$28.00	$13,280	517.14
Year 2	$1.04	$538	$30.00	$13,818	535.07
Year 3	$1.12	$599	$32.00	$14,417	553.79
Year 4	$1.20	$665	$34.00	$15,082	573.35
Year 5	$1.28	$734	$36.22	$15,816	593.62
Total	$5.60	$3,016			

As the above shows, Aggregate Cost on the account statement increased with each dividend payment and subsequent reinvestment. The cost increases equaled each year's dividend amount.

---

* Share increase calculation: dollar amount of dividend divided by the assumed share price equals number of shares

Over the five years, Aggregate Cost increased from the initial $12,800 to $15,816 at the end of 2017. This happened despite the fact that the investor had not contributed new money to buy the shares; the PFE dividend provided the funds.[**]

Now to the confusing part. At December 31, 2017, my friend's Pfizer investment had a value of $21,500.92 (593.62 shares x $36.22 = $21,500.92). Looking at the cost of the shares carried on the account statement of $15,816, one would calculate a gain of 36%. If, however, the look back was to the actual cash cost to the owner of $12,800, then the gain was 68.0%. The difference between the two is the amount of dividends reinvested (plus a slight profit on shares purchased with dividend payments).

No matter the accounting, the pre-tax economic gain on the original 500 Pfizer shares was an excellent 68.0%, 13.6% per year using a non-compounded average.

Reinvesting dividends and stock bundle distributions affects the cost of positions shown on monthly statements. When calculating the total profits on a stock, exchange traded fund or mutual fund position, make sure to refer to the aggregate cost for purchases funded with the owner's money. Do not include the cost of shares purchased with dividends or distributions.

[**] Technically, the presentation of increasing cost is accurate as each dividend reinvestment increases the investor's tax basis in the PFE position. Accurate, but confusing.

3

Time

Time is the investor's best friend. The longer one holds investments, be it stocks, bonds, or real estate, the more likely it is that a profit will be posted. This is particularly true for stock investments: the longer a diversified portfolio of stocks is held, the greater are the chances of making a profit. Time also benefits the stock investor relative to bond investors as longer holding periods increase the odds of stock profits exceeding those of bonds.

As has been discussed, the average yearly return of the US stock market is about 10%, including dividends. We also know that the market fluctuates around that average by about 18% in one year periods (its standard deviation). Putting the two together means that an investor can reasonably expect a return of between a positive 28% and a negative 8% in most years. It also means that in about 16% of the remaining years the percentage profit received will be higher than the range and in a separate 16% of the time the profit experienced will be lower than the range.

Clearly, the stock investor must be prepared to experience a negative result. How often has the US stock market posted down years? As the following data illustrate, the market has declined a lot less than most believe.

Introduced in 1957, the S&P 500 Index is the most widely used benchmark for the performance of the US stock market. The

194

Index represents the aggregate market value of an evolving group of 500 large US companies that in turn reflect the performance of the overall US economy. In the 61 years from its inception through 2017, the S&P 500 Index has produced a positive result, including dividends, in 47 years and a negative outcome in 14 years. The investor holding for one year was successful -- defined as receiving a positive result -- 77% of the time.

Over the same 61-year period, the S&P 500 suffered a cumulative loss (including the impact of dividends) in only two 5-year stretches. Purchasing a S&P 500 Index fund on January 1, 1973 and selling it on December 31, 1977 would have generated a loss in value of about 2% (before fees and taxes). Had the S&P 500 been bought on January 1, 2000 and sold on December 31, 2004, a portfolio loss of approximately 11% would have resulted.

These two negative results represent just 4% of the 56 rolling 5-year periods from 1957 through 2017. Thus, the historical odds of a positive profit for the S&P 500 Index investor with a 5-year time horizon were 96%, significantly higher than the 77% positive odds for a one year hold.

Red Alert: The average investor should avoid any financial engineering or exotic financial product that imposes a time limit or an expiration date on their capability to hold stocks. Most particularly, employing excessive amounts of debt to purchase stocks should be avoided as excessive borrowings limit an investor's capacity to withstand sudden or significant market declines.

Time also benefits the stock investor relative to the bond investor.

The upside for investing in stocks versus bonds is meaningfully higher profits over time. The downside is that stock prices fluctuate in a much wider range than do bond prices. How often should a stock investor expect stock profits to lose to bonds? The data shown below compares the stock market's performance relative to the bond market for the period from 1871 through 2012.[*]

Holding Period (Years)	Stocks Beat Bonds (% of Years)[*]
1	61%
2	64%
3	69%
5	69%
10	78%
20	96%
30	99%

As the above chart illustrates, the stock investor can reasonably expect to generate a profit exceeding that of the bond investor about 60% of the time assuming a holding period of 2 years or less. With a 3-year minimum holding period, stocks have won about 70% of the time. Holding for twenty years or more, stock profits have exceed bond profits over 95% of the time.

Stock market values have gone up in substantially more years than they have gone down. Stocks have generated consistently

[*] Siegel, Jeremy J., *Stocks for the Long Run.* 2014. Fifth Edition, page 94.

higher profits than bonds. Over extended periods of time, stocks are a better deal than bonds despite higher price volatility.

Time is your best friend when investing in stocks with the objective of creating wealth. Combined with a solid strategy, patience wins.

4

The Enemy

Human emotions are our biggest enemies when investing. Many get nervous before starting any new, unfamiliar process, especially so when the process involves their wallet. Most intensely hate losing money. Some get physically nauseous when the stock market drops suddenly. Take a deep breath. Feeling seasick in the uncharted waters of investing is normal.

Understanding what to expect emotionally from the different stages of an investing program is important, as managing through anxiety and uncertainty is critical to staying the course. Anticipating the emotional swings does not eliminate gut wrenching moments, but it is certainly helpful.

Opening the Capital Account: Dread

Most experience severe dread just taking the first step - opening a brokerage account. *Webster's Dictionary* defines dread as "anticipating with alarm, anxiety or reluctance." Even those who clearly grasp the financial benefits of opening a wealth-creating capital account often delay and procrastinate. Worse still, a sizable percentage of well-intentioned would-be investors yield to anxiety and never complete this stage. Since they are never in the game, they lose the opportunity to build financial strength.

Reasons cited to me over the years for procrastination or avoidance include: "I have never done it before." "I do not understand

and am afraid to make a mistake." "What if I have a question?" "I am comfortable with my bank." "I work all day and do not have time." "I'll get to it someday." "You need a lot of money to start." Interestingly, I very rarely hear, "I do not have any money."

None of these are valid excuses. Opening an account with Fidelity or Charles Schwab is simple, fast, can be done online 24 hours a day and toll free telephone assistance is available for questions. For companies like Fidelity and Schwab, new customer relationships are the lifeblood of their business. As a result, they make the new account opening process easy and painless.

Notwithstanding these truths, if dread still keeps you from taking the first step, walk into a Fidelity or Charles Schwab street store location and have a representative walk you through the steps. If your town does not have such a store, find a friend or relative that has an account and ask them to sit with you while you answer the questions on the web site. My son has performed this service several times for friends who wanted to get started, but were leery of making a mistake.

Overcoming the debilitating dread of opening a brokerage account is an absolute requirement for investing in higher earning stocks and bonds.

Choosing Investments: Terror

Be confident and proud. By opening an account, you have avoided the biggest and most costly mistake -- sitting on the sidelines.

The next step is to choose actual investments from among the thousands of options.

If opening a brokerage account incites dread, that dull, achingly anxious feeling, then picking a stock, stock bundle or bond fund without any guarantee of success incites more extreme feelings. The prospect of potentially losing hard earned money escalates the heart rate; the new investor rapidly moves from dread to the more intense emotions of fear, panic and terror.

You have plenty of company. Research by behavioral economists has shown that the typical investor hates losing money twice as much as they enjoy making money. Making matters worse, today investors get to experience losses in real time on their smartphones. Watching one's money "disappear" in a cascade of flashing red numbers as you stare at the screen is unnerving and scary for anyone.

At its core, this book is about building financial confidence and overcoming normal investing fears. Knowing a little market history, average yearly market returns and the odds of success of certain investment strategies goes a long way to reducing anxiety. Being able to put market moves in context is valuable and calming. With information, logical and profitable choices can be made.

The odds of success are quite good if you stick to the basic principles described herein. Following these principles does not guarantee uninterrupted year-after-year gains; no investing strategy works 100% of the time. Without doubt, the investor must be prepared for surprising and sudden fluctuations in prices and an account value which declines in some years.

Knowledge alone, however, is inadequate. The investor must combine knowledge with what I call "investing tenacity" and the guys in class started to call "money tough." Money tough is a combination of unwavering commitment, discipline and patience. When the down year occurs, being mentally tough and resilient will permit the investor to stay calm, turn off the smartphone and stay the course.

LIVING WITH MARKET HIGHS AND LOWS

The typical investor's emotions fluctuate with the fluctuations of the markets.

Bull Markets: Elation and Overconfidence

When the market is going up, investors are happy. They are confident about the future and all news is interpreted in a positive light. They love to talk about their winning stock picks at cocktail parties and backyard barbecues. Everyone from market gurus to Uber drivers know that the market will go even higher. Making money is easy. The economy booms as the wealth effect kicks in and consumer spending increases, reinforcing the positive environment. In short, investors are elated.

Be aware that this elation can lead to arrogance and overconfidence. During a bull market, many tend to become enamored with their investing prowess, taking personal credit for rapidly increasing account values and assigning no credit to the raging bull.

This happened to me early in my career as a Financial Analyst. I began work on Wall Street in 1982 just as one of the longest running bull markets in US stock market history began. With my limited salary, I bought a few stocks. Everything I bought went up. Picking winning stocks was easy and, after a few months, I was sure that I was the next great stock picker. I got so arrogant that one day I bragged to my boss about my success. He was an older man, a grizzled Wall Street veteran. With a deadpan look, he responded, "Youngster, let me give you a piece of advice. Do not confuse a bull market with brains." That comment certainly put me in my place.

As stupid as his comment made me feel, it was excellent advice. When the bull is running, be happy that your account value is increasing, but do not get caught up in the hype. Just because all positions are flashing green on your account screen does not mean you are a brilliant stock picker. Nor is it a reason to alter radically your investment parameters. Be cognizant of this natural inclination towards overconfidence and be aware that overconfidence can lead to risky investment behavior, such as making bets on highly speculative companies or strategies and using excessive amounts of margin debt.

Bear Markets: Fear and Pessimism

When the market is in a downward trajectory, investors are scared. Brokers worry about clients dumping them. Newspaper headlines in large, bold print scream out the big daily drops. The 24-hour news networks feature experts incessantly discussing the downward move. Excessive pessimism is the prevailing mood: no news is perceived as good news. Investors refuse to buy stocks, even ones they recently purchased at far higher prices. Second guessing is rampant. The politicians in Washington want to blame someone: Who is responsible for this mayhem? To end the pain, many capitulate to the hysteria and sell -- often very near the bottom.

To be sure, living through a bear market is unpleasant and requires stamina. Reading about or studying market downturns pales in comparison to experiencing them firsthand. Even the most seasoned investors feel uneasy in the face of flashing red numbers on the computer screen day after day after day.

Unfortunately, bear markets and corrections - respectively defined as 20% and 10% declines in the market from a previous high price - are a part of investing life. There is no avoiding these times. Do not look to the government for help as no amount of regulation or government monitoring can prevent markets from going down and occasionally going down dramatically. Note that the average bear market has lasted for only 19 months. For the investor, especially one experiencing the bear's claws for the first time, 19 months can feel like 10 years.

Here too, the best advice is to ignore all the overly-theatrical pessimism. Realize that newspapers and news shows have an incentive to overdramatize events because it pumps up their sales. When getting nervous, always refer back to the basics. Owning a stock is owning a company. Owning a stock bundle is owning a bunch of companies. Have all the businesses gone bankrupt or is it that the value Wall Street is placing on them has declined? Understand what you own. Understand why you own it.

Focus on the Long Game

Ignore recent events in the market and focus on a longer-term time horizon. Do not overemphasize more recent, less comprehensive information at the expense of longer-term, more complete data.

Time is your best friend, increasing the odds of investment success with the passage of each week. The typical institutional investor may have a one year time horizon and significant employment pressure to meet a yearly benchmark. You do not. The best way to deal with the roller coaster emotional highs and lows of the equity markets is to ignore the noise and mania. Put a long-term investment plan in place and be money tough.

5

Profits on Profits

Hopefully, at this point the logic is clear and compelling to:

- *INVEST:* Create wealth and a second source of income by opening and investing a capital account.

- *BE AN OWNER*: Invest a significant percentage of the capital account in ownership assets (stocks).

- *BUY BUNDLES*: Invest primarily in bundles for simplicity, diversification and tax deferral.

- *STAY STRONG*: Be money tough to stay the course, letting time be your best friend.

The last piece of the wealth creation puzzle is the imperative to reinvest cash flow received from stocks, bonds and bundles. Think: "profits on profits." Profits on Profits means that all cash flow from investments stay in the capital account and are invested in new securities. The account's value grows geometrically in the future as profits accrue on both monies previously deposited and on prior years' gains.

THE POWER OF PROFITS ON PROFITS

If there is a magical formula or an investing secret that rich, money smart people follow it is this one. To grow wealth most quickly, plow profits back into more profit-making investments. Be careful not to allocate money needed in the short run to the capital account because the rule is to never, ever withdraw funds.

The finance industry jargon for this process of reinvestment is compound interest.

Albert Einstein, the Nobel Prize winning physicist, was a big fan of compound interest. Apparently, he referred to it as "the eighth wonder of the world" and also called it the "most important invention of all time." Accurate quotes or not, the fact that Einstein is mentioned frequently in the same breath as compound interest hints at how meaningful this strategy can be to the investor.

Another pretty smart fellow and arguably the best equity investor of all-time, multi-billionaire Warren Buffett, attributes his financial success to "a combination of living in America, some lucky genes, and compound interest."

To explain the concept in class, I use the analogy of a snowball rolling downhill in a Saturday morning cartoon. With each turn, the snowball picks up new snow (new cash) and gets bigger (account value grows). As it gets bigger, the snowball rolls faster downhill picking up more snow (increasingly more new cash) on its larger surface (original investment plus past profits) and as its downhill speed increases more quickly with the larger mass, it grows larger and larger and rolls faster and faster (account value grows geometrically).

When profits, reinvestment and time come together, the results can be staggering and are often hard to believe for those new to the math.

The table below shows what $10,000 grows into at various annual rates of return compounded for three time periods.

Profits on Profits

Annual Rate	10 Years	30 Years	50 Years
Assumed Inflation:			
2.2%	$12,400	$19,200	$29,700
12.5%	$32,500	$342,400	$3,611,000
10.0%	$25,900	$174,500	$1,173,900
5.0%	$16,300	$43,200	$114,700
1.0%	$11,000	$13,500	$16,400

Several points need to be made based on the table. First, purchasing a bank Certificate of Deposit or parking in a savings account earning 1.0% per year is nearly worthless -- even if the investor stays the course for 50 years. At that rate, the investor gets poorer with each passing year and decade.

Second, even compounding at a pedestrian yearly rate of 5% for a long time -- 50 years -- turns a little into a lot. $10,000 grows to a respectable $114,700.

Lastly, the numbers get truly impressive when compounding stock market-type returns for a long time. Assuming the historical S&P 500 total annual return of 10%, $10,000 compounded for 50 years becomes nearly $1.2 million. Assuming the possibly higher return of 12.5% when employing a **Cheap & Strong** port-folio, the investor able to stay on track for 50 years turns $10,000 into about $3.6 million.

Note that the above results happen when investing a lump sum of $10,000 without making additional cash contributions. If new funds are deposited each year, then the growth in value is sub-stantially greater.

A smart strategy to accelerate growth is to deposit new cash each year equal to 5% of the account's beginning balance. Doing so turns a 5% investment strategy into a 10% annual growth in value or a 10% strategy into a 15% annual compounding factor.

Adding a consistent percentage of the beginning balance each year significantly speeds up the Double Time of your capital ac-count. For example, a 5% investment strategy that becomes 10% with 5% added from cash flow turns a 14.4 year Double Time into 7.2 years -- half as long.

After putting the Profits on Profits chart on the whiteboard in class, I typically get sarcastic eye rolls from the guys, quickly followed by questions and doubting comments. Some of the usual ones are: "Who can invest for 50 years?" "That is unrealis-tic." "I won't live that long." "I can't spend any of that money? Ever?" "Those numbers must be wrong." All are legitimate.

The future is unknowable and without guarantees. Wealth crea-tion is a journey of uncertain length and final destination. Investing, particularly in ownership assets, requires leaps of faith at almost every decision-making point. For example, the stock investor must trust that over long periods of time the historical relationship between stocks and bonds will continue. The small company stock investor must have faith that the **Smaller is**

Bigger strategy will continue to be rewarded with higher profits in return for lower liquidity and higher volatility. The **Cheap & Strong** investor must believe that investor psychology and behavior will continue as it has in the past, creating the value and momentum premiums. While likely, none of these are guaranteed.

Do not make the mistake of underestimating investment holding periods. Is 50 years of compounding realistic? It certainly is for an American 30 years of age or younger with the prevailing average US life expectancy of about 80 years. It is also a realistic duration for monies invested on behalf of young children or grandchildren. For those over 30, compounding for 20, 30 or 40 years is awesome. No matter the age, do not obsess on a particular time frame. Invest in a sound strategy and stay with it for as long as possible.

Do not fixate on a particular yearly profit number. Historical averages and numerical assumptions made in this book should be considered indicators of potential and not precise, expected targets. Stock markets go up and down on a seemingly random basis and no one can foresee what actual, realized profits will be. Be clear what the stock investor is betting on: that stocks will do better than bonds and that both will deliver more than inflation.

While the rule is to never, ever withdraw funds from the capital account, life can be messy. Serious issues may necessitate tapping into the account. When such issues arise, give ground grudgingly. Borrow against the capital account before liquidating positions and paying taxes. Alternatively, only use the annual cash flow or a portion of annual cash flow until the problem is resolved. Do not touch the capital base if at all possible. Upon resolution, get back on the profits on profits program quickly.

Red Alert: Absolutely resist raiding the capital account for non-essential expenditures.

The investor does not have to be as smart as Einstein or as financially savvy as Warren Buffett to harness the magical power of compound interest. Make sound investment choices. Reinvest cash flow and make additional contributions frequently. Check the impulse to withdraw money from the capital account for as long as possible, letting the magic of compound interest work. Religiously following this process guarantees a great result -- just not one that can be estimated precisely.

To the four imperatives for wealth creation listed above, add the final piece of the program -- NEVER SELL.

- Invest

- Be an Owner

- Buy Bundles

- Stay Strong

- Never Sell

6

Commitment Equals Success

Complete the action items described in this book and you will become financially stronger. More than likely, you will become rich if you follow the formula long enough. Certainly, your growing financial resources will facilitate more and better choices at every point in your life, likely contributing to increased happiness and lower levels of stress.

The key to success is an unwavering commitment to the process. You must consistently execute the formula: contribute some of every paycheck to the capital account, invest in ownership assets, and, most importantly, give investments the time to produce optimal profits. Do not waste time worrying about or calculating precise numerical goals. The magic of profits compounding year after year will take over and the money in the capital account will multiply beyond your imagination

Epilogue

Fantasy football is extremely popular in a Federal prison for men, with a significant percentage of the population participating. A few years in, I got involved. When I first joined, I felt like I was playing in a dense fog because the Commissioner did not explain the league's scoring system. After getting a copy of the scoring rules, I started to track game statistics and calculate points generated by every player. Gathering the numbers showed how to maximize my scores by drafting or trading for players favored by our system. As a result, my performance improved substantially and I won the league title several times.

A couple years after starting, the existing Commissioner was released and I took over his responsibilities. Because of my initial experience trying to compete without the rules, I made sure that every player received a copy of the scoring system so competition was fair and equitable. During my tenure as Commissioner, the players who tried to maximize their scores through application of the rules did well. Those that did not take the time to understand the scoring system did not win very often.

My fantasy football experience explains why I wrote this book.

As in a fantasy football league, everyone in the US plays in the same financial system by the same rules. Unlike optional fantasy football leagues, everyone is required to participate in the US economy; no one can decide not to play. If everyone must play, then I believe everyone should be given a chance to win.

Building wealth is not a mysterious process or an impossible task. Success is likely. I hope that many read this book in order to understand the rules and learn how to win.

Teaching the rules in the confusing language of Wall Street is not good enough, however. Experience taught me that people need a translation in order to learn and be compelled to action. My phrases, analogies and stories communicate the message more effectively. When guys nod their heads in agreement instead of nodding off, I know a translation hit home. When guys ask for advice outside class hours, I know I am getting through. Translation is essential to reaching the greatest number of people and motivating them to act.

"I wish someone had told me this earlier" is the most consistent comment I get from my students. When I hear this, I have a bittersweet reaction. In the first instance, I am gratified because it means that particular student got the message and has hope for an improved life after release. I am never more pleased than when I get a question about setting up a capital account for a child. Like me, that inmate wants to contribute positively to his child's life even from behind the prison fence. My second emotion is sadness. Here is a 30, 40 or even 50-year old man who was never given a roadmap to financial success. How different would his life have been if he had been shown a constructive, legal way to get ahead? How many of these guys would have taken a different life path? I pray that my students follow through upon release and improve the quality of their lives.

I am thankful that teaching my children investing fundamentals has enabled me to have a positive impact on their lives despite our separation. I am happy to report that all three are on their way to financial independence, one is employed by a prominent securities firm and the youngest recently graduated from college with a finance degree. Even better, this book has been a family effort requiring frequent communication. Their insights on content, editing of initial drafts and formatting the manuscript were invaluable.

Readers, tell your friends about the opportunity that exists. Share the Wall Street translations found here and encourage them to take immediate action to improve their financial strength.

Remember: Don't Waste Time. It's a Crime.

Acknowledgements

Sarah, Jack and Nick, thank you for your work creating this book -- nearly impossible without you and certainly not as much fun.

Thank you to the students at Camp Snoopy and at FCI La Tuna for being a great audience to test ideas. To name a few and with apologies to those I have neglected: G, Stevo, Tony the Tiger, Ian the Viking, Crazy Mike, Junior (who inspired the term bundle), Big Country, Beach (lover of the word scooping), Chase, CNN, Don Vito, Good News, JoJo, Chop Chop, Snooki, Marty, JB, Squirrel, Moose, Canada, the Alaskans, Dovey P, Nelly, Dino, Weezy, Kilo, Jughead (aka McLovin), Jesse, Goondabhai Kahn, Mr. Wie, Loc, Potter, Toot, Ryan, Boo, Sean, Joe L., Magic Mike, Stewie, Clear and Flashione.

Special thanks to Indian Joe for the Roadside Scholar name.

Ms. Brown, Supervisor of Camp Education, your sincere and tireless efforts to prepare the guys to reenter society and your positive energy were appreciated by all. Thank you to Ms. Kmetz at FCI La Tuna for the opportunity to teach.

Thank you to the folks who helped shape content and fix grammar: Marc, Sigrid, Rod, Noel and their daughters, Dan, #52, and Beth and Jim.

Thank you to Beth and Patti for the newspapers, magazines and books.

To Wayne (aka Rev Dirt), that first 14 hour, 2 day visit changed my life and continues to create positive reverberations. Your encouragement to write about my experiences is a big reason this came about.

Thank you to my snail mail pen pals. Practicing the lost art of writing letters was fun and therapeutic.

Thank you to a special person whose intervention returned me to family months sooner.

Finally, thank you to the over 100 people (an unofficial record) who sacrificed family time and made the long trip to visit over the years. You cannot possibly imagine how much inmates appreciate visits; they are the good days. Your support kept me sane.

When at the end of a prison sentence, particularly a long one, most get "short timer's disease." Short timer's disease is characterized by a complete loss of patience accompanied by annoyance with everyone and everything associated with being incarcerated. This project was a great antidote.

Appendices

Appendix A
Stinn Case Summary

Background: From September 1992 until November 2003, I was the Chief Executive Officer of Friedman's Inc. ("Friedman's" or the "Company"). Friedman's was unique with its strategy of opening jewelry stores in small towns in shopping centers typically anchored by Walmart. Using that approach, Friedman's grew rapidly from approximately 50 stores in 1992 to over 700 in 2003. An important element of the Company's business model was financing the jewelry sales of customers using its proprietary credit system; approximately 55% of revenue derived from credit sales. During this period of rapid expansion, Friedman's made net profits in every fiscal year. Profit margins fluctuated, however, as the performance of new stores and new geographies were inconsistent.

Genesis of the Legal Case: In 2003, a large jewelry manufacturing company, Cosmopolitan Gem, went bankrupt. Shortly after, a civil lawsuit was filed by Capital Factors, Cosmopolitan Gem's lender, accusing the principals of Cosmopolitan Gem and the senior financial personnel at several of its retail customers (specifically both the Chief Financial Officer and the Controller of Friedman's) of conspiring to defraud Capital Factors. In September 2003, the Securities and Exchange Commission launched an investigation into the allegations in the Capital Factors lawsuit which was followed by a Department of Justice probe.

After first vehemently denying the allegations, the CFO and Controller of Friedman's admitted their involvement in the more than $20 million Capital Factors fraud.

I was never implicated in or charged with any involvement in the Capital Factors case.

Get Out of Jail Free Card: The lawyers for the Friedman's employees advised them of the standard practice in the Eastern District of New York at that time -- the get out of jail free card. To eliminate or significantly reduce their jail time for the Capital Factors fraud, they needed to implicate someone else, preferably a higher up, in some type of criminal activity. If they could and later testified against that person, then they could skate on jail time.

Friedman's CFO and Controller had one problem: no one else at Friedman's had been involved in the scheme.

To remedy this, they made allegations of accounting impropriety at Friedman's and further that I was aware of their illegal activity. This allegation kicked off a years long investigation to find a crime.

Accounting Case Becomes Disclosure Case: The SEC and DOJ cases against Friedman's began with allegations of accounting manipulations. To be clear, there were no allegations of fraudulent transactions, only that the accounting for bona fide transactions was wrong. Later the case evolved to become a disclosure case as the critical fact in an accounting case -- materially inaccurate financial statements -- could not be proved.

DOJ Indicts in 2007: After nearly 4 years of investigation and hundreds of interviews, I was indicted in 2007 by the Department of Justice. Unlike most accused by Federal prosecutors, I chose to go to trial to prove my innocence.

SEC Passes: The SEC never brings an enforcement action or lawsuit against me after years of investigation.

2008 Trial in Brooklyn Federal Court: During a seven week trial, the DOJ alleged that Friedman's made disclosure violations in its filings with the SEC that materially harmed the investing public and that I was responsible.

Specifically, they claimed: 1) The word "generally" in the description of the Company's charge-off policy was not descriptive enough of its practices (particularly the accepting of bona fide credit payments after fiscal month end -- what they called "scooping"); 2) The word "strict" as used in the Form 10K in a Risk Factor and again in the Credit Operations section of the Business Description was inaccurate; 3) A computer malfunction resulting in impaired credit accounts receivable (the "X Files") was reserved for at too low an amount and not disclosed; 4) The reserve for future credit losses was inaccurate; and 5) A tax payment made by Friedman's on behalf of five members of the executive management team was not properly approved by the Board of Directors (despite the fact that it wasn't scheduled to be until a later meeting).

Both the CFO and the Controller testified at trial to fulfill their bargain. They attempted to cast a sinister light on every decision in order to make conduct seem criminal. Mission accomplished: both received probation for their involvement in the massive Capital Factors fraud instead of years in prison.

Holdout Juror: After days of deliberating, the jury could not come to a unanimous decision. One juror had doubts. After she was pressured by her fellow jurors and the presiding judge, a guilty verdict was delivered. Immediately after the verdict was rendered, the jury was polled individually as per standard practice. During polling, juror #10 stated that she did not agree with the verdict. In most cases, such a statement would result in a mistrial. In this case, the judge refused to grant a mistrial. Instead, the holdout juror was removed from the panel and a substitute who had witnessed the events was empaneled.

Convicted March 2008: A guilty verdict for securities fraud was rendered shortly after the new juror was added.

Missing Element: One of the four necessary elements of a securities fraud crime is the existence of the theft of property, more commonly called the "loot." There is no crime unless something is stolen. In my case, since I had never sold a share of stock, the loot requirement was satisfied by either 1) my Board approved increase in salary for one fiscal year and bonus in the same year, or 2) the shareholders' intangible right to information. Since the jury was not required to agree unanimously on the loot element, the nature and amount of property deemed to have been stolen was never precisely determined.

Sentencing 2009: In April 2009, I was sentenced to 12 years in Federal Prison and required to pay millions of dollars in restitution (such restitution has since been deemed illegal pursuant to the Supreme Court's Lagos decision in 2018).

Prison: I reported to the Federal Correctional Institution near El Paso, Texas in June 2009. I was transferred "on the chain" (shackled on "Con Air" and BOP buses) to a Federal Satellite Camp in Northern California in November 2010 where I served until released to a residential reentry center in San Francisco, California in April 2019.

Appendix B
Double Double

In advanced classes, we play Double Double, a version of Double Time that includes both the annual contribution rate from deposits (the savings rate) PLUS an assumed rate of return on a capital account's investments (the investment rate). Actively managing both elements -- contribution rate and a portfolio's targeted return -- will generate the best results with the fastest double times. What is particularly helpful with Double Double is the feedback it provides in terms of portfolio construction.

The calculation: 72 divided by the sum of the rate of savings deposited into the capital account PLUS the assumed annual total profit on the portfolio.

For example, begin with a five-year Double Time that requires an annual savings/deposit rate of 14.4% (72/5 = 14.4%). Saving at that rate will double the account value in about 5 years.

To play Double Double add an expected annual rate of profit produced by the portfolio to the 14.4% savings rate. Note that adding ANY investment profits will speed up the expected time to a double.

Assuming the account is invested in a CD paying 1.0% per year, the Double Time speeds up to approximately 4.7 years from the original 5 year goal -- marginally faster.

Assuming the account is invested in a 30-year US Treasury security with a yield of 3.0% per year, the Double Time speeds up even more to about 4.1 years -- quite a bit faster.

Assuming the account is invested in stocks exclusively with an average market return of 10.0% annually, the Double Time decreases to just about 3 years -- a lot faster.

To increase the Double Time even more, the deposit rate would need to be increased because assuming more than a 10% return is too aggressive. For a two year double with an assumed 10% investment profit, the savings rate would need to be about 26% per year. (72/(26% + 10%) = 2 year double).

The above calculations show the impact of investing in CDs -- some benefit but not much, a Treasury that exceeds the inflation hurdle -- a nice benefit, or the stock market that builds wealth and purchasing power the fastest.

In the advanced class, each student is asked to calculate their Double Double as a check after deciding on an asset allocation strategy for a capital account.

To achieve the fastest Double Time, manage both the savings rate and a capital account's investments. Playing Double Double helps set targets and enlighten the investor on portfolio allocation decisions.

Appendix C
Company Valuation Ratios

Investors value company shares by comparing a stock's price to measures of that company's economic production. In so doing, investors can fairly compare companies of different sizes and in different industries.

Having a basic understanding of valuation concepts is helpful for the individual investor. Knowing how to execute the precise calculations and the theories underlying each ratio is not required. Know that a lower valuation ratio relative to a company's economic production means a faster payback for the shareholder and generally a higher profit from owning the stock.

Price-to-Earnings (P/E ratio): The ratio of a company's price divided by its yearly profit (earnings per share). The P/E ratio is expressed as a multiple, 12x for example. A handy way to understand P/E is to substitute "years" for the little "x" in the multiple. A 12x multiple, then, is a 12-year payback absent any growth in profits. Paying lower purchase multiples for comparable assets generally results in better investment profits.

Earnings Yield: The earnings yield is the inverse of the P/E ratio, calculated as yearly profit divided by the price paid and expressed as a percent. For example, a P/E of 12x translates to an earnings yield of 8.3%. This means that the company earns profits of 8.3% of the share price per year, assuming no earnings growth. Using this relationship, a higher percentage is better.

Earnings yield is often used to compare stock valuations to bonds by calculating what is called the equity premium (also referred to as the risk premium) for a stock versus a bond. For example, if the 10-year US Treasury bond is paying interest of 3.0% per year and a stock has an 8.3% earnings yield, then the equity premium is 5.3%. This is the additional amount the investor is getting paid to assume the greater risk of holding an equity security versus a US Treasury obligation. For the broad US market, the equity premium has averaged approximately 3% historically.

Price-to-Sales (P/S ratio): The ratio of market value to the company's annual sales, expressed as a multiple. The P/S ratio determines how a company is valued relative to its entire economic output, regardless of profitability.

The P/S ratio is calculated using a company's total market capitalization divided by its total sales. As an example, if a company has a $2.3 billion market value and generated $1.0 billion in sales for the prior year, then its price-to-sales ratio is 2.3x. One can also think of this as paying a price equal to 2.3 years of sales. Lower ratios are generally better values.

Price-to-Book Value (P/B ratio): The ratio of a company's price in the market to its financial statement net worth or book value. The accounting concept of net worth or book value is the excess of what a company owns (total assets) over what it owes (total liabilities). Book values in the aggregate and on a per share basis are disclosed by all public companies. A lower ratio is more favorable.

Corporate income and cash flow can vary from year to year, but book value is fairly stable. Using the P/B ratio as a valuation metric is particularly appropriate when companies are operating at peak cyclical profitability or recession levels of profitability.

Price-to-Cash Flow (P/CF ratio): This ratio compares the price paid to a company's cash generated by operations. This calculation is appropriate when comparing companies of differing capital intensity or companies that have timing issues between accounting profits and cash profits. A lower P/CF multiple is preferred.

EBIT-to-Total Enterprise Value (EBIT/EV ratio): This relationship is a bit more esoteric and not discussed as often in the financial press. It compares operating profits (earnings before interest expense and taxes) to a company's total capital employed (market capitalization plus total debt), expressed as a percent.

It is used to arrive at a company's profit generating capability irrespective of the relationship of equity to debt financing in its capital structure. A higher percentage means the company earns a higher profit per dollar of capital used in the business.

Price-to-Earnings Growth Rate (P/G ratio): Earnings drive stock prices. To be more precise, expectations of future earnings drive stock prices. To get at this concept in terms of valuation, the analyst compares the current valuation to the company's expected earnings growth rate. Accurately assessing a company's growth prospects is critical to the calculation.

Dividend Yield: Investors also look to dividend yields to compare companies, particularly companies of the same size and in the same industry. To arrive at the dividend yield, divide the amount of a company's per share annual dividend payments by the price paid per share and express the result as a percent. Among comparable companies, a higher cash dividend yield -- more cash returned to the owner per dollar of cost -- is generally viewed as a better deal.

Appendix D
Glossary

Bases Loaded: A nickname for a portfolio of ETFs using the market benchmark outperformance themes discussed herein: small company, value, momentum and bonus bundles.

Bear Market: A 20% decline from a previous market high.

Bid/Ask Spread: The difference between the prices at which market makers will buy (bid) or sell (ask) a stock or other security. The spread amount is a cost to the investor.

Bond: A loan issued by a government or a company pursuant to a contract that commits to repay borrowed money at a fixed rate of interest at a specified time.

Bonus Bundles: Equal Weight or Fundamental Indexing stock allocation strategies.

Brokerage Firm: A company in the securities industry that buys, sells and holds investments on behalf of clients.

Buffett Allocation: A portfolio allocation between stocks and bonds advocated by Warren Buffett: 90% S&P 500 Index bundle and 10% bond bundle.

Buffett Plus: The Buffett Allocation with an Equal Weight S&P 500 Bundle replacing the S&P 500 component.

Bull Market: Market conditions in which prices are rising and typically exceed prior highs.

Bundle: A package of stocks or bonds wrapped together for convenience of purchase by investors.

Capital Account: A brokerage account opened with a reputable securities firm devoted to the production of wealth for the owner of the account.

Cash Flow: Money from one's paycheck minus expenses paid out; calculated for a finite time period (e.g. month or year).

Cash is King: A nickname for Fundamental Indexation strategies, including the Dogs of the Dow strategy.

Certificate of Deposit: A certificate issued by a bank for depositing money for a specified length of time that earns interest for the depositor, typically at a rate higher than a savings account.

Cheap & Strong: A nickname for a portfolio that combines the value and momentum (relative price strength) styles of investing.

Compound Interest: The addition of income received by the investor to the principal sum of an investment which is also then invested. Reinvesting annual income, rather spending it, means that income in future periods is earned on an ever growing sum.

Consumer Price Index: The statistic issued by the United States government that measures price changes at the consumer level.

Correction: A 10% decline from a previous market high.

Coupon: The rate of interest paid on a bond is usually fixed. The dollar amount paid is the coupon amount or just the coupon.

Credit Risk: Credit risk is the possibility of a loss resulting from a borrower's failure to repay; the risk that a lender may not receive contractually owed principal and interest resulting in an interruption of cash flow.

Deflation: A decrease in the average level of consumer prices.

Diversification: A risk management strategy that mixes investments within a portfolio in an attempt to generate a higher risk adjusted profit compared to holding one or a more limited number of investments.

Dividend: A dividend is the income an investor receives from owning a stock or another dividend-yielding asset. Typically, dividends are paid on a quarterly basis.

Dividend Reinvestment: A strategy in which a cash dividend is used to automatically purchase more of the underlying investment.

Dividend Yield: The annual dividend divided by the cost of the stock expressed as a percent. It represents the rate of current income an investor receives from owning a stock.

Dollar Cost Average: A strategy in which an investor buys the same dollar amount of an investment at regular intervals, regardless of the asset's price, to neutralize short-term volatility.

Double Time: The calculation of the amount to save per year to double one's money. Divide 72 by the amount of time to double to determine the amount of cash savings required per year.

Exchange Traded Fund: A collection of securities bundled together for convenience of purchase. ETFs can contain many types of investments, including stocks, commodities, bonds, or a mixture of investment types. An exchange-traded fund is a marketable security with an associated price that trades on an exchange.

Fixed Income Security: A fixed-income security is an investment that provides a return in the form of fixed periodic interest payments and the return of principal at maturity.

401(k) Account: An investment account intended for retirement savings sponsored and managed by an employer pursuant to IRS regulations.

Full Service Broker: A brokerage firm whose principal business is advising clients on an individual basis as to appropriate investments and portfolio design, and then performs the buy and sell trades.

Globetrotter: A nickname for an ETF portfolio combining a US Cheap & Strong component with an international bonus bundle component.

Go With the Mo: A nickname for the momentum or relative price strength style of investing.

Guaranteed Losing Account: A bank savings account in which cash is left for too long a period of time.

Have it Your Way: A philosophy of prioritizing expenses to fit each person's unique value system.

Human Emotion: The enemy of investors.

Individual Retirement Account ("IRA"): A tax advantaged brokerage account opened by an individual (e.g. not sponsored by an employer) in which the investment decisions are made by the individual.

Inflation: An increase in the average level of consumer prices.

Inflation Hurdle Rate: The minimum annual rate of return that an investment must exceed to create purchasing power and wealth for the investor.

Interest: The income received on a fixed income security.

Interest Rate Seesaw: The relationship between interest rates and bond prices: as one goes up, the other goes down.

Investor's Profit Equation: Price increase (decrease) of the security (stock, bond or other) plus the amount of dividends or interest paid less commissions and fees on trades.

Liquidity: An assessment of an investment's cash conversion characteristics. How long does it take and at what cost can an asset be converted to cash in pocket?

Market Bundles: Exchange traded funds or mutual funds that replicate the components of a market index, such as the Dow Jones Industrial Average, the S&P 500 or the NASDAQ Composite.

Market Capitalization: The total price the stock market places on a company: the number of shares outstanding multiplied by the current price of a share.

Money Tough: A combination of unwavering commitment, discipline and patience to a chosen long-term investment strategy.

Mutual Fund: A collection of securities bundled together for convenience of purchase. Mutual funds are operated by professional money managers to match a stated investment objective. Mutual funds do not trade on an exchange.

Net Asset Value ("NAV"): The value of the holdings of a mutual or exchange traded fund on a per share basis. The NAV is the price at which mutual fund investors buy and sell once per day.

Online Broker: A brokerage firm whose principal business is facilitating self-directed trading over the internet for clients.

Par Value: The stated value of an issued security as opposed to its market value. Par value equals the redemption price for bonds.

Pay Less, Get More: A nickname for the value style of investing.

Price/Earnings Ratio: The price-to-earnings ratio (P/E ratio) is the valuation ratio that measures current share price relative to per-share earnings (EPS). The price-to-earnings ratio is also sometimes called the earnings multiple.

Price Fluctuations: The up and down movement of prices as securities trade.

Profits on Profits: A nickname for Compound Interest.

Rating Agencies: Companies which provide investors with consistent credit information that assists in determining whether issuers of bonds and other fixed-income securities will be able to meet their obligations.

Rebalancing: The process of realigning the weightings of a portfolio of assets. Rebalancing involves periodically buying or selling assets to maintain a desired level of asset allocation.

Regular Brokerage Account: An account opened with a securities firm with after-tax dollars that bestows no special tax advantages to the account owner. Often referred to as a taxable account.

Smaller is Bigger: A nickname for an investment style favoring small and mid-size companies over large companies.

Standard Deviation: A statistical tool that measures the spread of a data series around the mean (average) value.

Stocks: Ownership interests in companies, typically public companies that trade on an exchange.

Tax Advantaged Account: Designed to comply with tax incentives built into the tax code, these accounts give certain income tax benefits to owners. Annual dollar limits apply.

Technical Analysis: A trading discipline employed to evaluate investments and identify trading opportunities by analyzing statistical trends from trading activity, such as price movement and volume.

Ticker Symbol: A public security or fund's unique alphabetic nickname by which it is identified and trades under.

Time: The investor's best friend.

Total Return: The investor's profit consisting of gain (loss) on sale or increase in value plus the amount of interest or dividends received, typically measured and quoted for annual periods.

Valuation Ratio: A mathematical calculation comparing the price of a security (e.g. a stock price) to a factor reflecting the relevant company's economic production.

Volatility: The up and down movement of prices as securities trade.

Yield to Maturity: Yield to maturity is the total profit anticipated by an investor on a bond if it is held until all principal is repaid. Yield to maturity is expressed as an annual rate. In technical terms, it is the internal rate of return (IRR) of a bond investment if the investor holds the bond until maturity with payments made as scheduled and reinvested at the same rate.

Bibliography

Bernstein, William J., *The Four Pillars of Investing,* Second Edition, The McGraw-Hill Companies, Inc., New York, New York, 2010.

Bernstein, William J., *The Intelligent Asset Allocator*, The McGraw-Hill Companies, Inc., New York, New York, 2001.

Bogle, John C., *Stay the Course: The Story of Vanguard and the Index Revolution*, John Wiley & Sons, Inc., Hoboken, New Jersey, 2019.

Brigham, Eugene F. and Daves, Phillip R., *Essentials of Intermediate Financial Management*, Cengage Learning, Mason, Ohio, 2009.

Fullenkamp, Connel Ph.D., *Understanding Investments: Course Guidebook*, The Great Courses, 2012.

Gray, Wesley R. Ph.D., Vogel Jack R. Ph.D., and Foulke, David P., *DIY Financial Advisor, John Wiley & Sons, Hoboken, New Jersey, 2015.*

Gray, Wesley R. Ph.D. and Vogel, Jack R. Ph.D., Quantitative Momentum: A Practitioner's Guide to Building a Momentum-Based Stock Selection Strategy, John Wiley & Sons, Inc., Hoboken, New Jersey, 2016.

Gray, Wesley R. Ph.D. and Carlisle, Tobias E. LLB, *Quantitative Value: A Practitioner's Guide to Automating Intelligent Investment and Eliminating Behavioral Errors*, John Wiley & Sons, Inc., Hoboken, New Jersey, 2013.

Greenblatt, Joel, *The Little Book that Still Beats the Market*, John Wiley & Sons, Hoboken, New Jersey, 2010.

Greenwald, Bruce C.N., Kahn, Judd, Sonkin, Paul D. and van Biema, Michael, *Value Investing: From Graham to Buffett and Beyond*, John Wiley & Sons, Hoboken, New Jersey, 2001.

Ilmanen, Antti, *Expected Returns: An Investor's Guide to Harvesting Market Rewards*, John Wiley & Sons, Ltd., United Kingdom, 2011.

Jakab, Spencer, *Heads I Win, Tails I Win*, Penguin Random House LLC, New York, New York, 2016.

Montier, James, *Value Investing: Tools and Techniques for Intelligent Investment*, John Wiley & Sons, Ltd., United Kingdom, 2009.

O'Shaughnessy, James P., *What Works on Wall Street: The Classic Guide to the Best-Performing Investment Strategies of All Time*, Fourth Edition, McGraw Hill, New York, New York, 2012.

Robbins, Tony, *Money: Master the Game*, Simon & Shuster, New York, New York, 2014.

Siegel, Jeremy J., *Stocks for the Long Run: The Definitive Guide to Financial Market Returns & Long-Term Investment Strategies*, Fifth Edition, McGraw-Hill Education, New York, New York, 1998.

Silver, Nate, *The Signal and the Noise: Why So Many Predictions Fail -- but Some Don't*, The Penguin Press, New York, New York, 2012.

Singal, Vijay, *Beyond the Random Walk: A Guide to Stock Market Anomalies and Low Risk Investing*, Oxford University Press, New York, New York, 2004.

Statman, Meir, *Finance for Normal People: How Investors and Markets Behave*, Oxford University Press, New York, New York, 2017.